Small Boat Sailing

Percy Blandford

Macdonald Guidelines

Managing editor
Chester Fisher
Series editor
Jim Miles
Editor
Alan Wakeford
Designer
Peter Benoist
Picture Researchers
Linda Proud
Jenny Golden
Production
Penny Kitchenham

First published 1978
Macdonald Educational Ltd
Holywell House
Worship Street
London EC2 2EN

Printed and bound by
Waterlow (Dunstable)
Limited

ISBN 0 356 06030 6

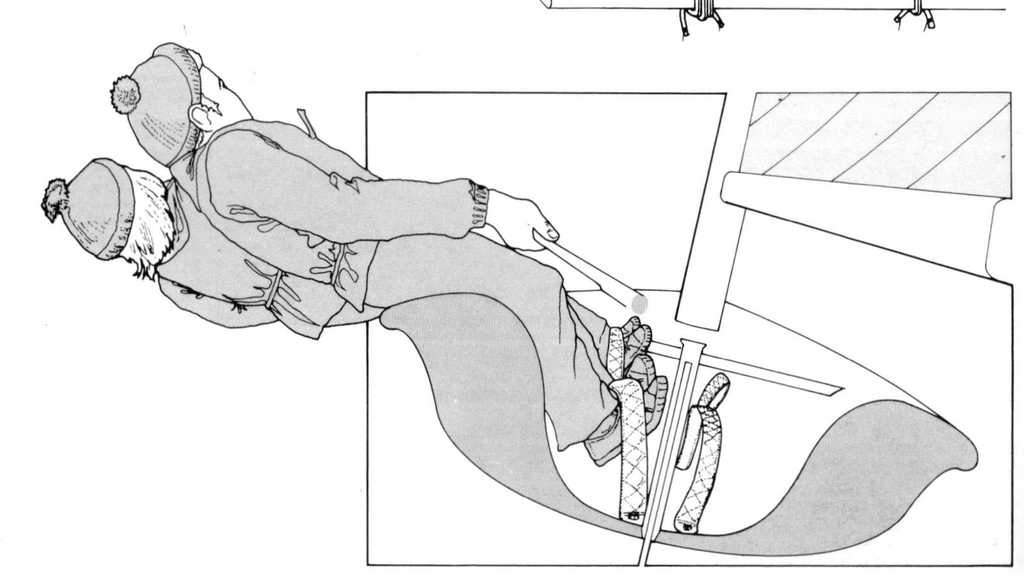

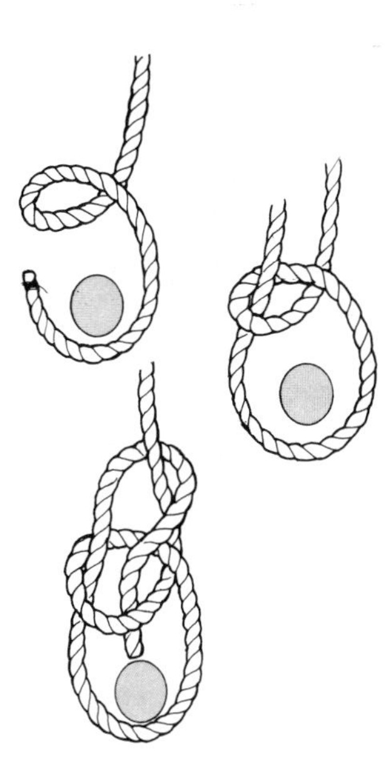

Contents

Introduction

Sailing is a recreation or sport available to almost everyone and facilities are becoming increasingly available on inland and coastal waters. For most newcomers to sailing the first boat is an open dinghy with a simple rig, while for the family man the boat may be partly decked. He may even choose a small sailing cruiser with cabin accommodation to provide snug overnight bunks, cooking and toilet facilities. Sailing a small cruiser is little different from sailing a dinghy. And that is what this book is all about.

Why sail?

Compared with other possible leisure activities, sailing has many attractions. A great deal of enjoyment is derived from harnessing the wind to drive a boat in the direction you wish. It doesn't take long to learn the basics of seamanship and from then on you can continually improve your techniques. The more you sail the more skilful you become at reading the wind and sea conditions. The wind is not a constant source of power and you have to make the most of its fluctuations and variations. And the feeling of skippering your own dinghy or cruiser is something that many people consider is without parallel. Sailing also offers a sense of exploration even if you arrive by boat at a place you may know quite well by the shore approach. For those with a competitive spirit, racing adds a new dimension. Skill and enthusiasm are necessary to master the course and in these circumstances you don't have to win to enjoy sailing.

With the increase in leisure time, the demands made on recreational facililities of all kinds have increased. However, the majority of waters have not yet become overcrowded although a few popular sailing places are congested at the height of the summer season. There is still plenty of other water to be used and those sailing offshore or even close inshore will be

◀ Early Egyptians knew about sails for use in a following wind. But they rowed their boats when the wind was in any other direction.

▶ In a modern cruiser, a family can enjoy the thrills of sailing combined with all the needs for comfortable living.

▶ Sailing merchant ships have gone, but tall ships live on as valuable training vessels particularly for young people. Their races are beautiful and nostalgic occasions.

surprised at how alone they can be for much of the time.

A growing recreation

The boom in sailing interest today is due to many factors. As the standard of living has increased more people can now afford to buy a boat. Even if they don't base the dinghy or cruiser at a yacht club on the coast or inland water they can very easily tow it by car to suitable sailing places at weekends.

The wherewithal to buy a boat, however, must be seen in conjunction with the tremendous improvements made in boat design and the materials used to build them. Many of these changes came about due to World War II. Really waterproof glues brought marine plywood into being. Then came glass reinforced plastic. In consequence the boat building industry was revolutionized—small boats could be produced in quantity for the first time. These improvements have now been supplemented by the use of aluminium alloys for

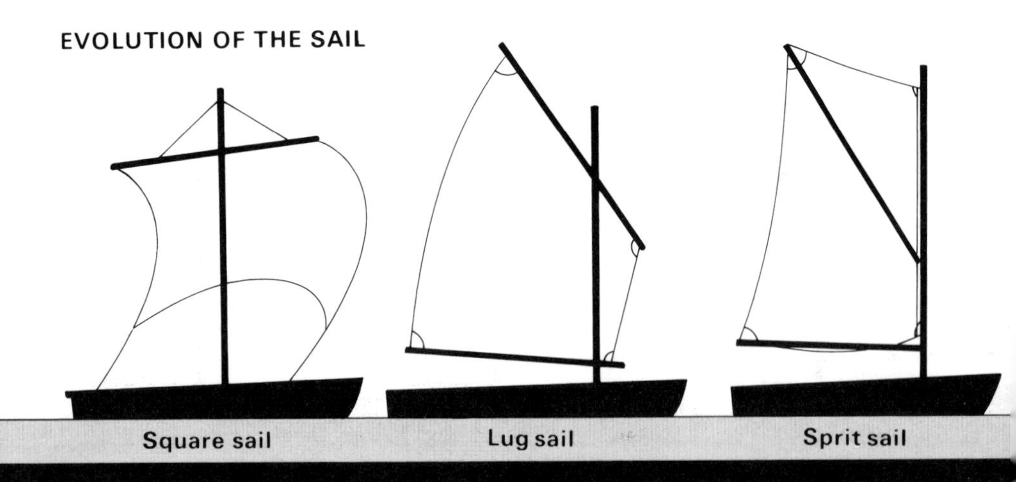

spars and synthetic fibres for ropes and fabrics.

The history of sail

The first sail was devised by primitive man for use on a canoe or raft. It was a makeshift affair and probably consisted of an animal skin suspended from a crossbar (yard) fixed to a mast. However, it had a limited use and acted as a respite from paddling only when the wind was blowing from behind. The idea that sails were solely effective within a few degrees of directly downwind persisted until comparatively recent times. The development of square sails, with a more sophisticated use of spars and sailcloth, allowed a sail to be positioned so that a boat could sail at an angle to the wind. But the shape of many hulls meant that boats still tended to drift downwind cancelling out any progress made.

Even up to the final days of sailing ships in the 19th century, boats had to wait for a fair wind before setting out. Adverse winds still made it virtually impossible to hold to a set course. Many hulls were designed as load carriers and did not have the correct shape to grip the water when the wind was blowing from the side (beam) of the vessel. Consequently any attempts to sail other than downwind resulted in considerable leeway.

More progress was made in the sailing ability of smaller craft, but except for British ketches, American trading schooners and a few other larger craft, the benefits of early aerodynamic knowledge were not applied to ships, which still had to have their voyages planned to benefit from 'trade winds'.

Sail shapes

The square sail hanging from a yard will drive a boat downwind as well as any other sail. If it is pulled round so the yard is at an acute angle to the centreline of the hull, it will drive the boat at a progressively closer angle to the wind. However such a loose-footed sail does not set very well and early experimenters added another spar to form a boom to tension the foot of the sail. They also found that performance was improved by increasing the angle of the yard upwards. This produced the balanced lug, which formed the basis of small craft rigs for a long time. With the boom brought

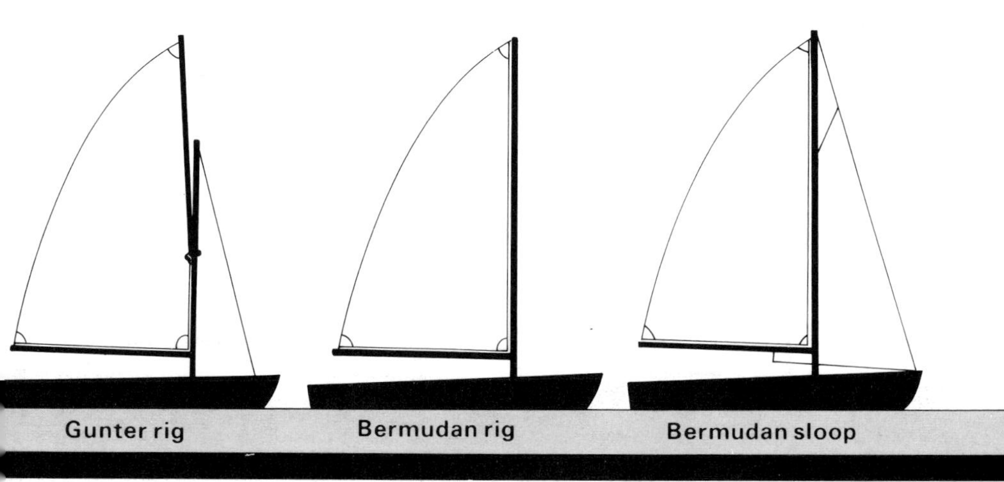

entirely behind the mast and joined to it with a gooseneck (a universal metal joint), the name changed to a standing lug.

Further sail developments brought the yard peaked even higher until it continued straight up the mast. This arrangement became known as the gunter rig and the next logical step was to let the mast go all the way up giving rise to the Bermudan mainsail.

One other way of dealing with a square sail brought fore-and-aft was to use a sprit going diagonally across the sail. This is still seen in a few dinghy classes, such as the Optimist, but the most famous application has been in the Thames barge. This had a very large mainsail which was never lowered, but the canvas could be gathered up by ropes called brails. It was the largest trading craft that could be handled by two men. Although none is still trading, there are still a great many being sailed as pleasure craft.

More than one sail

Besides changing the shape of sails experiments were made using more than one sail. It was found that sails forward of a single mast aided in manoeuvring a boat. There were similar benefits from having another mast and sail aft. Such results led to a proliferation of sails and during the 19th century this developed almost into an obsession. The trend was encouraged by the inability to make and support very tall masts, so a spread-out sail plan broken into many parts overcame this structural problem.

There is a fascination about these complicated rigs but it is generally recognized that sails are more efficient if the total area is kept to a minimum number of sails. Furthermore the taller the rig is, within reason, the closer a boat can sail to the wind. This is the reason why nearly all modern small craft have a tall mast and Bermudan mainsail and one foresail.

Variations on a theme

The development of sailing craft in all parts of the world has not followed the same course, although the same principles have been discovered and applied. The Chinese junk, for example, has battens across its sails, which are kept more rigidly to shape than Western sails. Versions of the junk rig

▼ Victorian yachts had low, long, divided sail plans, while the Chinese concentrated their sail area into one fully-battened sail.

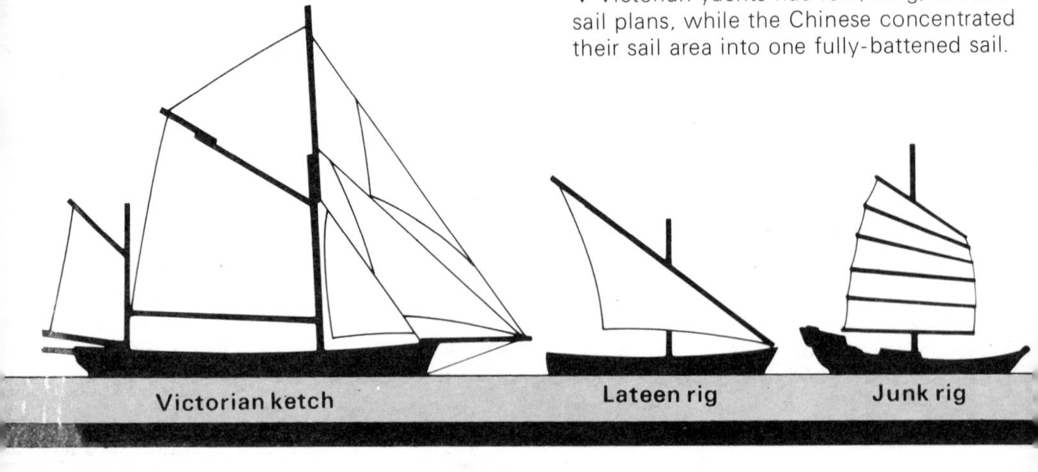

▲ Old gaff-rigged yachts are picturesque, but the long spread of canvas is not as efficient as the same area in a modern high rig, nor as easily handled.

have been used on Western cruising yachts with some degree of success, including several long ocean voyages.

Normal sails tend to push the bow down. There is an advantage in a lifting sail, particularly in a beam wind. Early Egyptian sailors on the Nile and Polynesians in the Pacific had mainly this type of wind to contend with and both evolved the lateen rig, which gives more lift than most other rigs.

Research into aerodynamics has shown that flexible cloth is not the best material for getting the most efficient sail shape. But so far no one has found a way of making efficient rigid sails that can be adapted to wind from either side. It may be that differences in sail construction will come, but much of the joy of sailing comes from watching and setting the flowing curves of canvas.

Principles of sailing

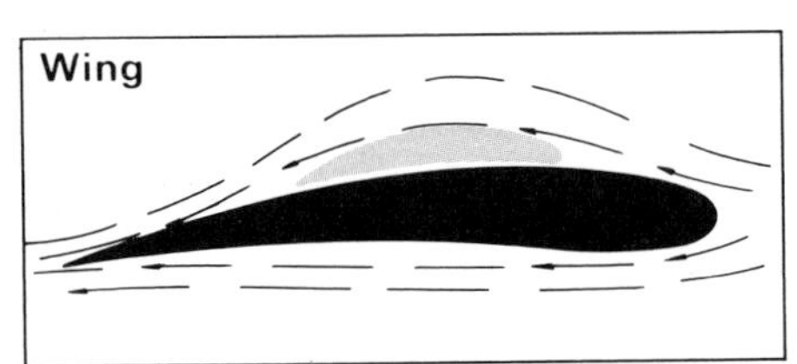

A sail going to windward gets much of its drive from the vacuum induced in a similar way to the airflow over an aircraft wing.

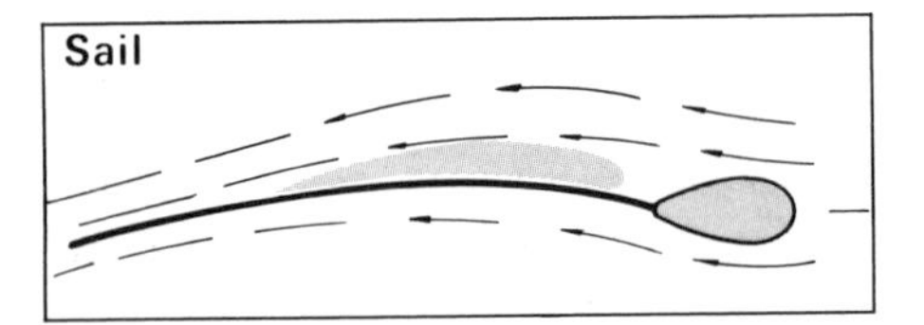

Using the wind to drive a boat is not quite as simple as might at first be thought. It is easy to understand why a boat moves forward when the wind is filling the sails from behind, but it is more difficult to appreciate the principles which enable a boat to sail close to the wind. Until the 20th century improvements in the shape of sails and designs of hulls had taken place slowly, mainly by trial and error. Now a far more scientific approach is used to produce more efficient sailing boats.

The propelling force

The sails are attached to the boat by rigging. As the wind acts on them the lines and spars comprising this rigging transfer the power to the hull and the boat moves forward. However, this is not a perfect arrangement. Some wind power is lost and the hull does not go in exactly the way it is pointing. Much of the skill and enjoyment of sailing therefore comes in making the most of the wind power, so that losses are minimized and the boat goes faster in the direction you want to travel.

Directions of travel

If a sail is across the boat and the wind is coming from aft, the boat is obviously propelled directly away from the wind. In fact this was the only situation in which early sailors used a sail. In any other direction they rowed or paddled or just waited for the wind to change.

If the wind approaches the sail from any angle other than directly aft, the reaction is different. When attempting to sail at an angle towards the wind, the sail and mast

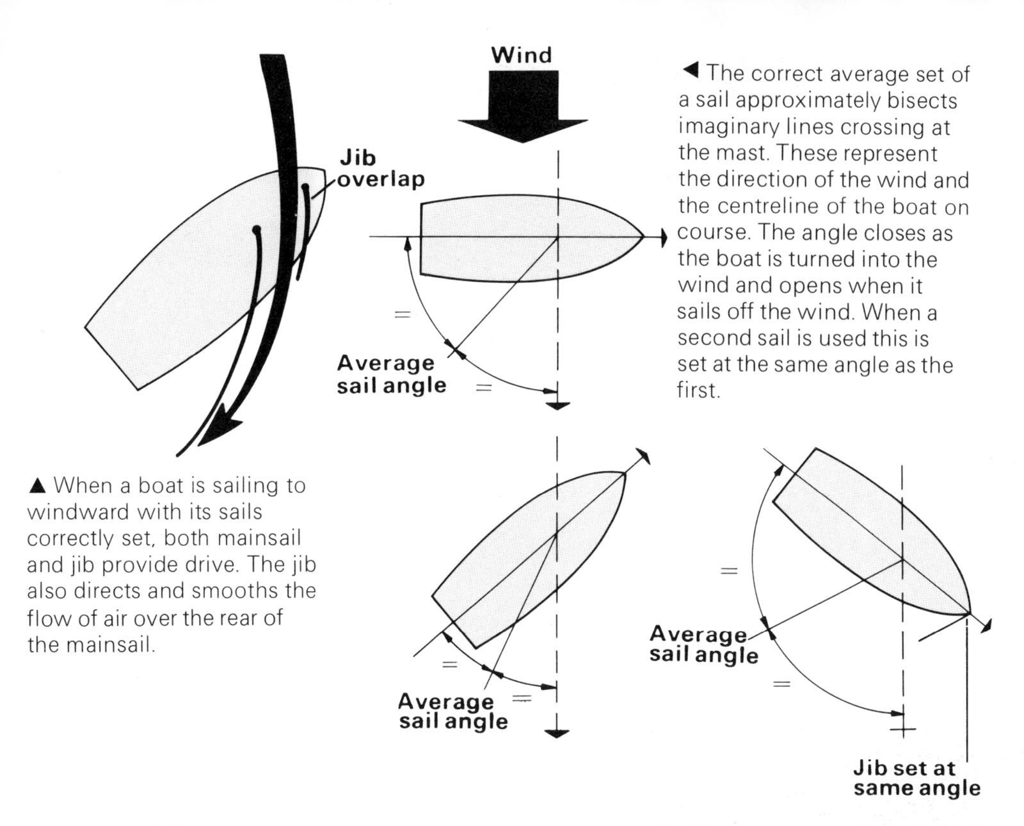

◀ The correct average set of a sail approximately bisects imaginary lines crossing at the mast. These represent the direction of the wind and the centreline of the boat on course. The angle closes as the boat is turned into the wind and opens when it sails off the wind. When a second sail is used this is set at the same angle as the first.

▲ When a boat is sailing to windward with its sails correctly set, both mainsail and jib provide drive. The jib also directs and smooths the flow of air over the rear of the mainsail.

are comparable to an aircraft wing being drawn through the air. Because of the shape of a wing section, a partial vacuum is created on the top side. The air pressure on the underside is consequently greater and so uplift results.

Consequently, the best set of a mainsail when going to windward should resemble, as near as possible throughout its height, an aircraft wing section. This is impossible with cloth, but it is the reason why modern rigs have much more pull down on the boom than older craft.

When aircraft had less powerful engines than they do now, greater uplift was created by fitting auxiliary surfaces in front of the wings. These directed air over the top of the leading edges via a slot. In likewise fashion, overlap of the jib on the mainsail can have a similar effect.

Setting the sails

Experienced helmsmen know where to set the sails in relation to the wind, principally by the 'feel' of the boat. But it may help a beginner to regard it as a geometric problem. This can only give an approximate result, but it is a help in first learning sail setting. Imagine two lines, one along the centre of the boat when pointed on its intended course and another in the direction of the wind crossing the first through the mast. The mainsail should be kept roughly at the angle that bisects them and the other sails set at the same angle as this. To get the correct average angle higher up the sail, the boom has to be pulled in slightly more.

As it points more towards the wind, the angle of the mainsail becomes more acute

DIRECTIONS OF SAIL

A boat may be sailed in any direction except directly towards the wind and in the sector about 45° either side of it. When the boat's attitude to the wind is as close as it can be sailed, it is 'close-hauled'. If the sheets are eased a little and it sails at about right-angles to the wind, it is on a 'reach'. And sailing further away from the wind takes it onto a 'broad reach'. When sailing directly downwind the boat is 'running'.

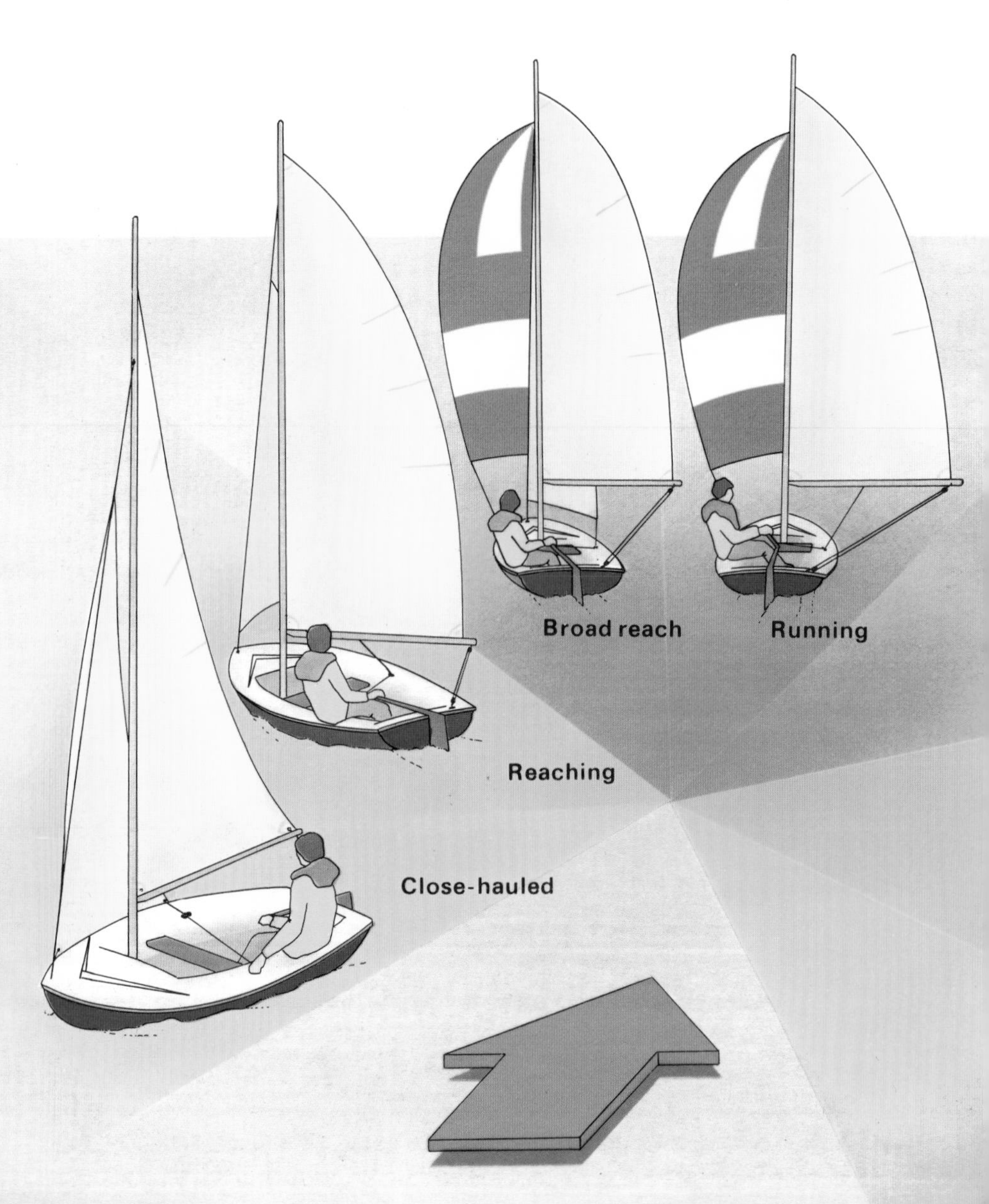

and the sail is hauled in further. As it points more away from the wind, the angle gets wider, until the boat is pointing directly downwind and the wind and course lines coincide. The sail is then set at right-angles to them.

The hull

A hull sitting on top of the water, like a raft, is liable to be driven downwind whichever way its sail is set. Therefore, it has to be shaped so that it goes forward through the water with minimum friction and resists being driven from its course. Consequently, it needs to be much longer than it is wide and have sufficient depth to grip the water. The underwater shape is most important, but too much hull projecting above the water can also affect sailing performance as well as stability. A small sailing yacht cannot have its cabin as high as on a motor yacht of comparable size, because of this.

The best waterline shape is pointed at both ends. Quite often the boat has another form above the water, but it should be trimmed so the intended underwater shape is not spoiled. A transom across the stern should be almost completely above the water. If the boat is down by the stern and much of the transom goes below the sur-

▼ This well-heeled yacht shows the easily-driven lines of a round-bottomed hull with a fin keel.

face, progress will be slowed by a drag effect. This is indicated by a turbulent flurry of water aft.

To prevent excessive drift or leeway in a beam wind, it is important that there is sufficient boat below the water. The hull itself may go deep enough, but in most small craft it is usually comparatively shallow. Consequently, extra keel surface is required. This could be a fin fixed permanently to the centre of the hull, a pair of fixed bilge keels, or leeboards over the sides of the boat. Alternatively, a lifting keel has the same effect. This can be either a daggerboard, lifting up and down in a central case, or a centreboard which swings up into a case.

The rudder is used to get the boat on course. It also helps to prevent leeway. When the boat is sailing properly, the rudder blade should be near central. If it has to be set far to one side, it induces drag and indicates that the sail plan is incorrectly balanced, the hull is badly trimmed, or the sails are wrongly set for the intended course.

Maintaining stability

A boat is designed to perform best when sailing near upright. The disposal of ballast is therefore important in maintaining stability. Sometimes the keel is weighted and so acts like a pendulum to keep the hull in the correct position in the water. However, such weight causes drag and this is not wanted. In a smaller boat, the crew act as movable ballast and so can be placed to counteract any heeling tendency due to the wind.

Factors affecting performance

The shape and size of a hull affect performance. Every hull has an optimum speed through the water. Once that speed is reached it takes an inordinate amount of power to make it go a little faster. A long hull has a higher optimum speed than a short one, so there is an advantage in length, even more than in other factors.

The hull shape that has the minimum wetted area, and therefore the minimum drag due to skin friction, is semi-circular underwater. As this is an unstable shape, the centre part of the section is usually flattened so it is like a D on its side. If the hull is made of plywood or other flat materials, the shape has to be modified to an angular section, but a rounded bottom should perform more efficiently. An exception is a planing hull. If a hull with a broad

▼ For the smoothest progress, the waterline shape of the hull should be pointed at both ends.

▼ The 'centre of lateral resistance' can be found by balancing a drawing of the underwater shape on a knife.

▼ Leeway is reduced by the underwater hull and rudder, as well as the actual keel.

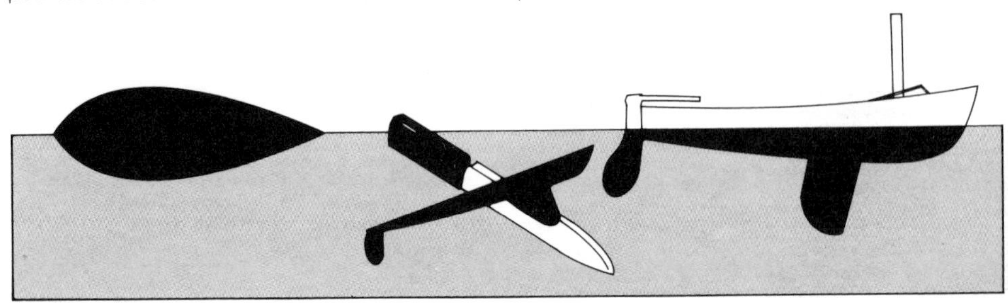

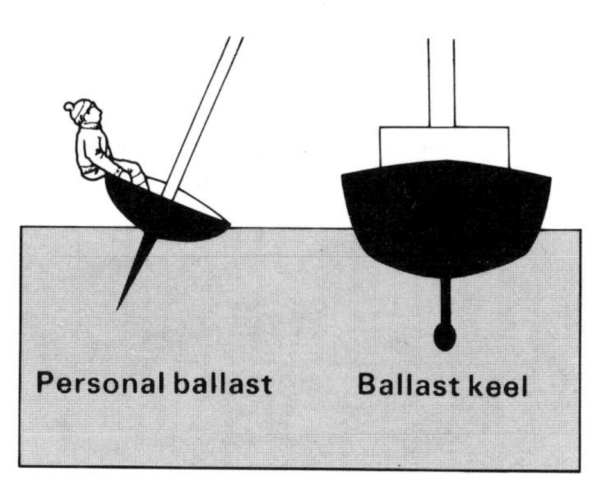

▲ Ballast for stability may be just the crew of a small boat or a weighted keel on a larger boat.

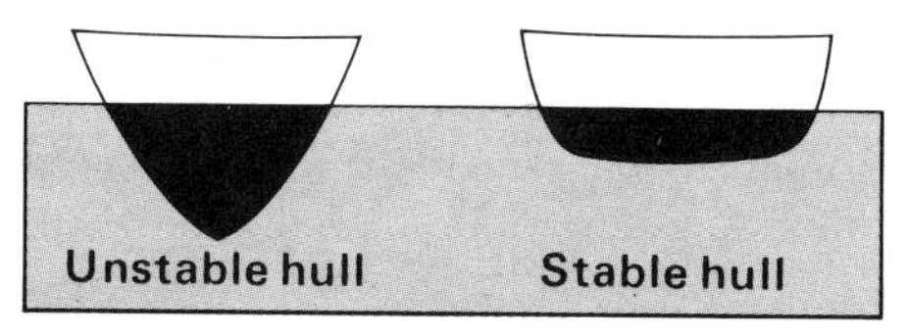

▲ The cross-section of the hull affects stability. A semi-circular or V section is unstable, but flattening the centre of a curve gives a stable shape.

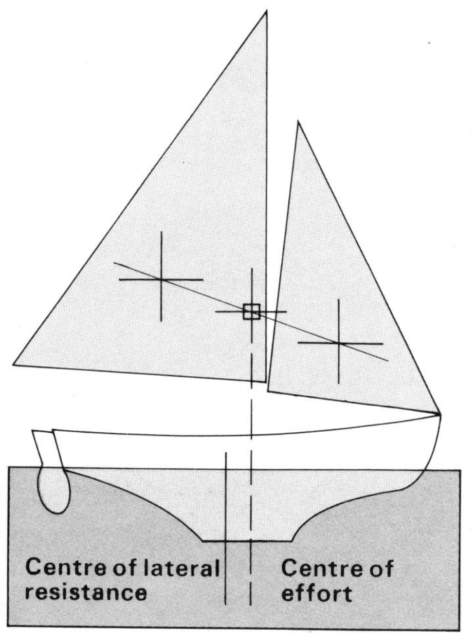

flattish bottom aft is driven hard enough to lift partly out of the water onto a plane, the wetted area is reduced and there is a considerable gain in speed.

Correctly relating the sail plan to the hull is the concern of the designer, but some knowledge of this may help a helmsman get the best out of his boat. Sails can be changed and the trim of the boat altered by moving weights, if the effect of these actions is understood. A floating hull pivots about a point of balance called the 'centre of lateral resistance'. This can be found by cutting out the shape of the underwater profile from card, so it can be balanced on a knife edge with the waterline at right-angles to the knife. The 'centre of lateral resistance' is on the balance line.

The point of balance at which all the wind pressure acting on a sail plan may be assumed to be concentrated is called the 'centre of effort'. This can be found geometrically by locating the centres of each triangle in the sail plan, and the combined effect is proportional to areas along linking lines (see drawing).

In motion, 'centre of effort' should be slightly aft of 'centre of lateral resistance'. The combined effect of boat movement and wind causes the 'centre of effort' to move aft and a designed position slightly forward of the 'centre of lateral resistance' gives a correct position when moving. Not much can be done to the centre of effort while sailing, but movements of the crew fore and aft in a small boat can have considerable effect on the location of the centre of lateral resistance.

◀ To achieve the correct relation of sail plan to hull, the combined centre of effort of the sails should be slightly forward of the centre of lateral resistance of the hull. In practice, the centre of effort moves a little aft of the centre of lateral resistance as the boat sails forward.

Sailing terms—general

There are a great many traditional names for the parts of a boat and its rig. The essential terms are given on these and the following pages, with explanations of more in the glossary. Many others from the great days of sail are now obsolescent. It is better to use plain language than archaic terms. Usage changes. For instance, most modern sailing craft are sloops, with only one sail forward of the mast. Today that sail is called a 'jib'. It has been known as a 'foresail' or 'headsail' and a purist might still insist on calling it a 'staysail'.

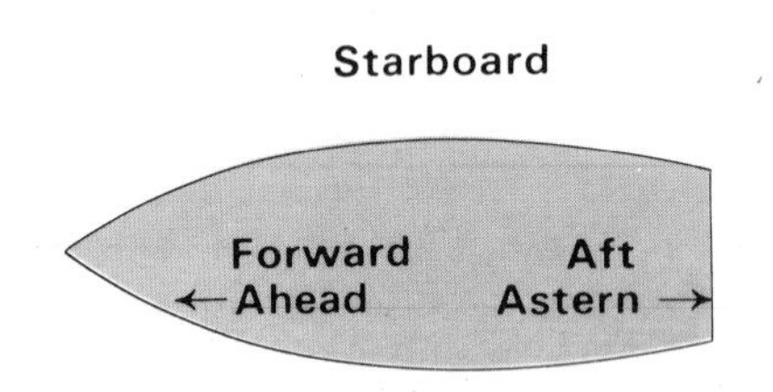

Directions on board

The port side is to your left and the starboard side to your right when facing forward. It is a help in memorizing to know that the two shorter words 'port' and 'left' go together. Before rudders were invented, a boat was steered by an oar over the side. As most helmsmen were right-handed that 'steerboard' was on the right. The location of the red and green navigation lights can be remembered by associating the red colour of port wine with the red port light.

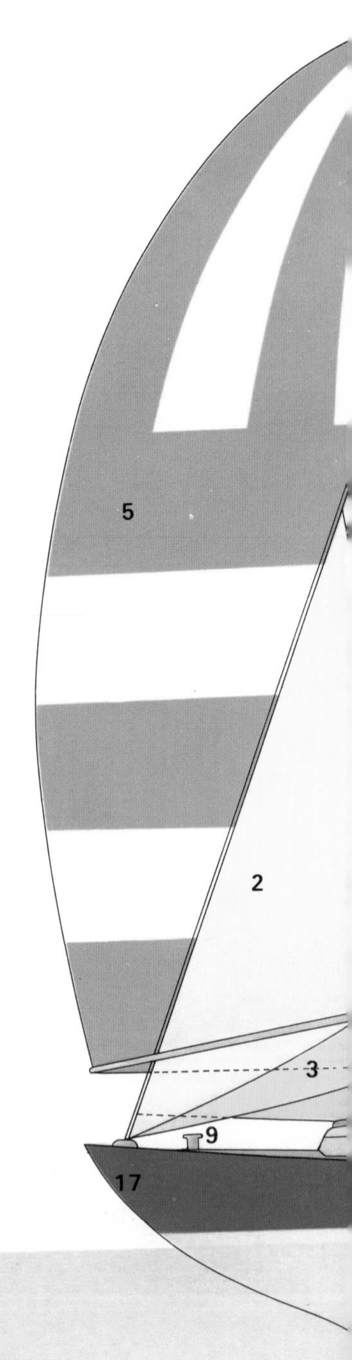

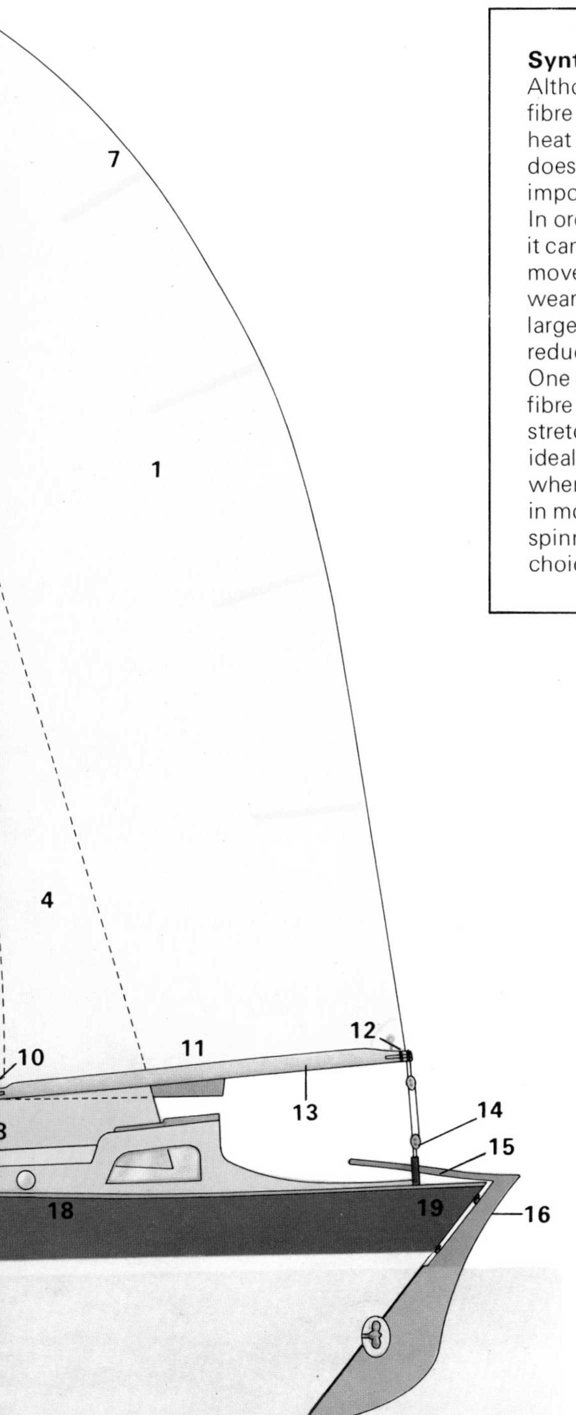

Synthetic fibre rope
Although more durable than natural fibre rope, it can be damaged by heat and it suffers from chafe. It does not rot, so dry storage is not so important, but keep it free from grit. In order that the rope wears evenly, it can sometimes be reversed or moved, so different parts take the wear or strain. Having sheaves as large as is reasonably possible reduces friction and wear on ropes. One great advantage of synthetic fibre ropes is that they do not stretch significantly and so they are ideal for most purposes afloat. But where an elastic rope is required, as in mooring and controlling spinnakers, nylon rope is a better choice.

Key
1 Mainsail
2 Jib
3 Staysail or foresail
4 Genoa
5 Spinnaker
6 Burgee
7 Battens
8 Mast tabernacle
9 Sampson post
10 Gooseneck
11 Foot
12 Clew
13 Boom
14 Horse
15 Tiller
16 Rudder
17 Bow
18 Amidships
19 Stern

Sailing terms—rigging

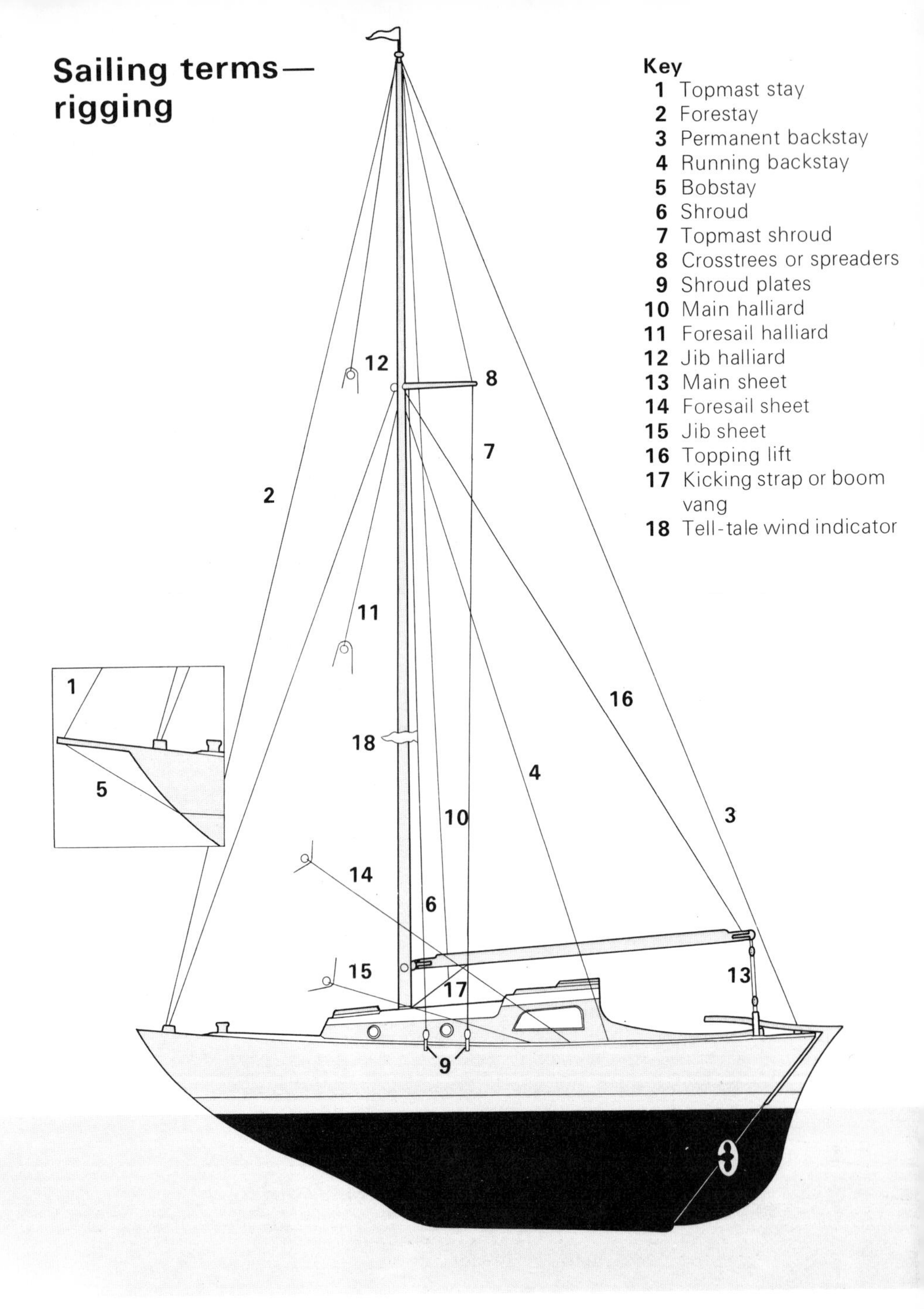

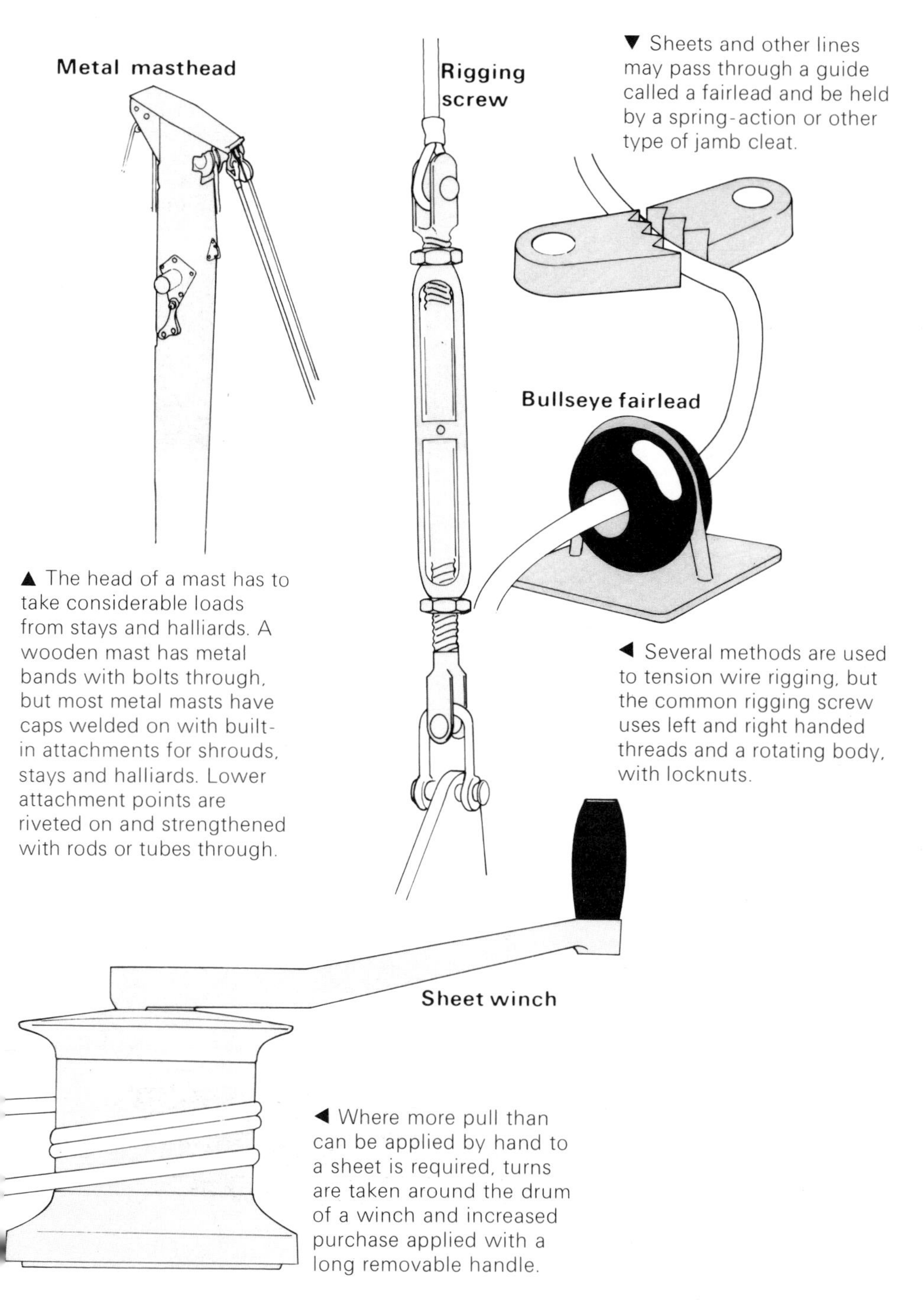

▼ Sheets and other lines may pass through a guide called a fairlead and be held by a spring-action or other type of jamb cleat.

▲ The head of a mast has to take considerable loads from stays and halliards. A wooden mast has metal bands with bolts through, but most metal masts have caps welded on with built-in attachments for shrouds, stays and halliards. Lower attachment points are riveted on and strengthened with rods or tubes through.

◀ Several methods are used to tension wire rigging, but the common rigging screw uses left and right handed threads and a rotating body, with locknuts.

◀ Where more pull than can be applied by hand to a sheet is required, turns are taken around the drum of a winch and increased purchase applied with a long removable handle.

Boatbuilding and sailmaking

Until comparatively recently, wood was virtually the only material from which boats were built. Now the availability of new materials, such as glass fibre, has revolutionized their construction, and plastic, nylon and stainless steel are used for fittings.

Boat construction using wood

Clinker (clench or lapstrake) planking This is one of the oldest forms of construction consisting of overlapping planks pegged together with wood. The Vikings even used this method for their boats which first crossed the Atlantic Ocean. More recent clinker planking has the overlaps joined at intervals with copper rivets. The boat is first assembled over temporary formers, then bent frames ('timbers') are put round the inside.

Carvel planking In this method the planks or 'strakes' are arranged flush on the outside. Sometimes glue is applied to the joints between the planks, but it is more usual to caulk by driving in cotton followed by a flexible compound. Traditional carvel

▼ A reinforced glass fibre mould for a bilge-keel cruiser, mounted in a cradle to permit tilting for ease in working.

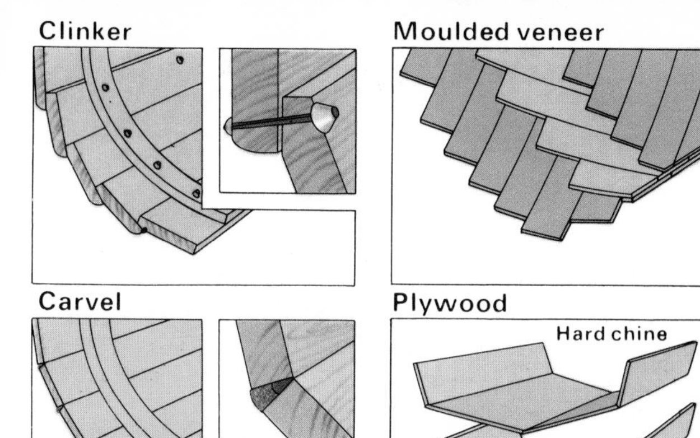

Types of wooden hull
A clinker hull has overlapping planks riveted together and bent timbers inside to provide stiffening. With a carvel hull, the planks are laid flush lengthways and the seams made waterproof. A longer process is to mould thin layers of wood into the required shape. But a plywood hull cannot be bent in the width as well as the length, so it has to have one or two angles (chines) between straight cross-sections.

planking makes a good sound boat. However, because a reasonable thickness of wood is needed to hold the caulking, it is unsuitable for smaller boats. Another method of making a flush skin uses narrow strips of wood glued and nailed or screwed to each other as well as to frames.

Moulding A good round-bottomed hull can be made by moulding very thin strips of wood over a temporary plug. Usually there are three layers, with the narrow strips in alternate diagonal directions. The terms 'hot-moulded' and 'cold-moulded' refer to the means of setting the waterproof glue between layers. The method makes a good, light, durable hull, which is low in material costs but very time-consuming to build. Other methods of building round-bottomed hulls use strips of wood or double skins glued diagonally. Some larger craft even have double skins with canvas between them.

Using plywood

One of the most popular materials for amateur boatbuilding is marine grade plywood (marked 'BSS1088' in Britain). However, it cannot be bent in two directions at once, so to make a boat curved in the length there have to be straight lines in the width. The simplest arrangement has a joint along the keel and only one angle on each side, called a 'hard chine'. A closer resemblance to a round bottomed hull is a 'double chine', with a narrow piece between two angles. A common method of building such shaped boats was to erect frames, stem and transom on the workshop floor in an inverted position. Strips were added lengthwise and the plywood skin fixed with glue and screws, or barbed ring nails. The method is still used, but now some dinghies are built with the frames only acting as formers. When turned over, the hull lifts off them and internal stiffening is built in using thwarts and buoyancy cases.

Another method of smaller plywood boatbuilding is usually called 'stitch and glue'. A good example is the popular Mirror dinghy. This does not involve setting up on frames. Plywood panels are cut to shape for all parts of the hull and holes drilled along the edges that are to meet. Adjacent panels are then brought together and tied with short pieces of

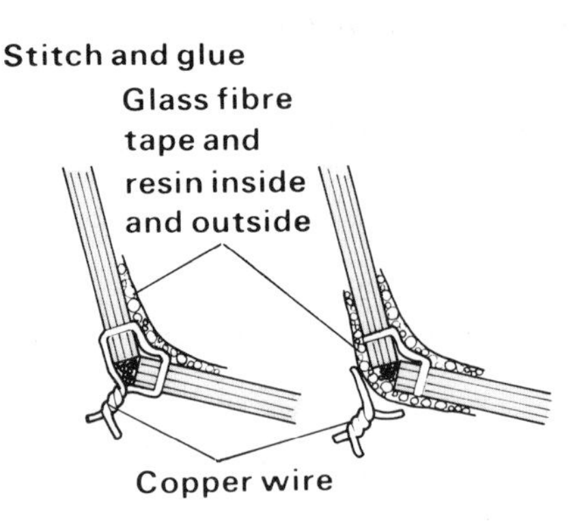

◀ The 'stitch and glue' method is a relatively simple way of building a hull from plywood. Wire loops, resin and glass fibre tape are used to join the panels with a watertight seal. The Mirror dinghy is one of the most popular boats put together in this way.

copper wire passed through the holes and twisted on the outside. The curved edges of the panels cause the hull to pull into the boat shape as they are wired. Glass fibre tape is laid in resin along the sides of the joints and left to set. The outside wire is cut off and the ends filed level, then more tape and resin are applied outside the joints and this holds and waterproofs them. There are no frames or other solid parts inside. The hull is stiffened by its deck, thwarts, bulkheads and buoyancy compartments. Most of the internal parts are fixed with resin and glass fibre tape.

Boat construction using glass fibre

Glass fibre construction is now the most popular method of making pleasure craft. It produces a tough, durable, one-piece hull. There is no risk of leaks and little maintenance is needed. The process is more suitable for quantity production than one-off amateur construction. However, moulds can be hired for some popular boats so a single hull can be made economically.

A plug has to be made in the shape the boat is to take. This is usually of wood and has to be brought to a good finish, as any imperfections will be reproduced in the final boat. The plug is coated with release agent, then resin and glass fibre mat are laid up over it. This will form the mould,

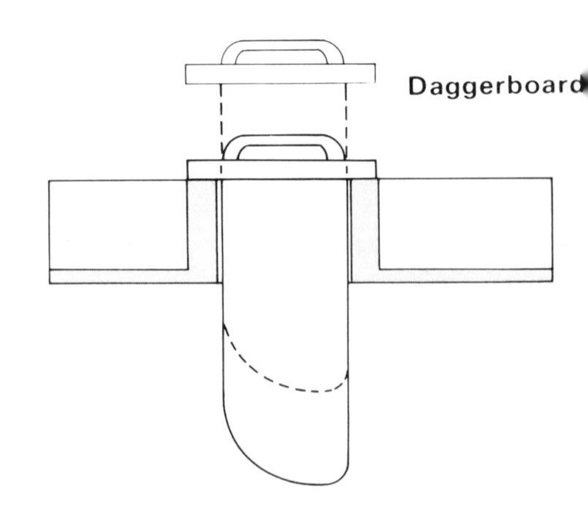

Daggerboard

Glass fibre moulding

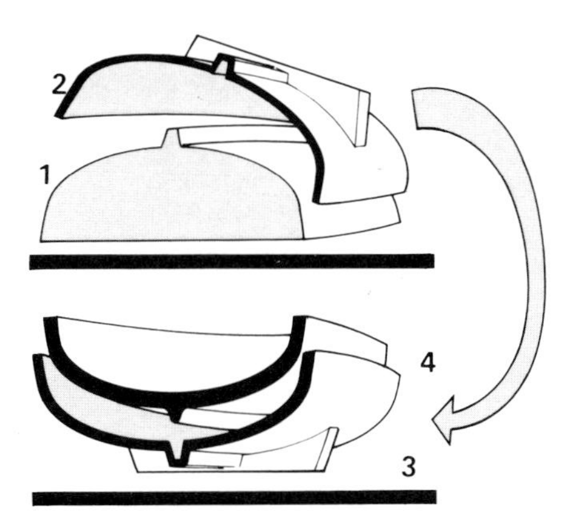

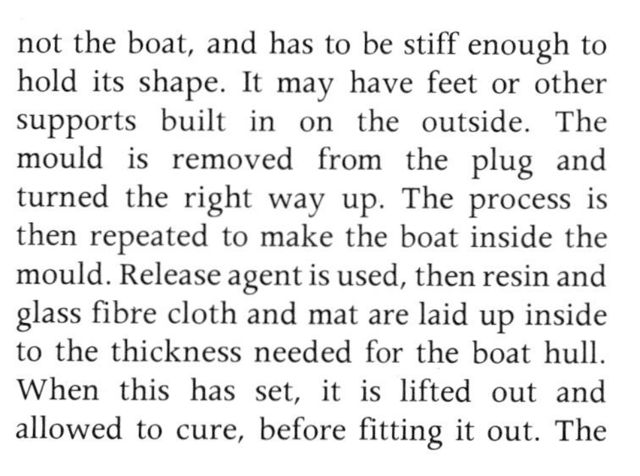

▲ The first step in making a glass fibre boat is a wooden plug (1), over which a glass fibre mould is made (2). This is turned the right way up (3) and the actual boat made inside it (4).

▲ Bilge keels allow a boat to sail in shallower water and to stand level when it takes the bottom at low water.

not the boat, and has to be stiff enough to hold its shape. It may have feet or other supports built in on the outside. The mould is removed from the plug and turned the right way up. The process is then repeated to make the boat inside the mould. Release agent is used, then resin and glass fibre cloth and mat are laid up inside to the thickness needed for the boat hull. When this has set, it is lifted out and allowed to cure, before fitting it out. The same mould can be used for any number of similar hulls. Plugs and moulds can be made for deck and cabin mouldings as well as other parts. Wood can also be incorporated in mouldings for attaching internal parts.

Plastics have been used for boat hulls and there are methods of combining plastic foam with glass fibre. New methods may develop, but the majority of boats are likely to continue to be made by the methods described.

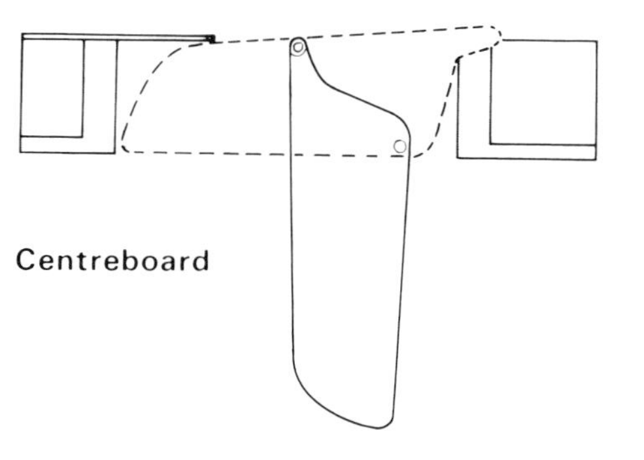

◄ A daggerboard or centreboard is used on a dinghy to reduce leeway as the boat progresses through the water. The daggerboard, found mainly on small boats, is held vertically in its case and is lifted and dropped by hand. An elastic shock-cord can hold it in any position, but when not required it can be removed from its case. The centreboard has a pivoting action with various arrangements of ropes and pulleys so that it can be raised and lowered.

Fitting out the hull

Masts and spars have traditionally been made of wood. Until the development of waterproof glues, they were mostly solid poles. Now they can be hollow and therefore lighter. Booms were made with two parts glued together to include a rope groove. Although wood masts are still used, many boats have aluminium alloy masts and spars which are mostly lighter and stronger.

Strong waterproof glues have made laminating the usual way of making shaped wooden parts. For example, the dogleg shape of a tiller may be built up with strips glued together. Knees that form brackets to stiffen corners and support decks may also be made in this way, instead of having to use wood with a curved grain. Boat fittings, such as cleats and fairleads, were usually galvanized iron or bronze. For small craft they are now either stainless steel, nylon or other plastic.

▼ For hand work on sails, there are many sizes of triangular pointed needles. These are used with stout thread and pushed with a 'palm' worn with the thumb through the hole.

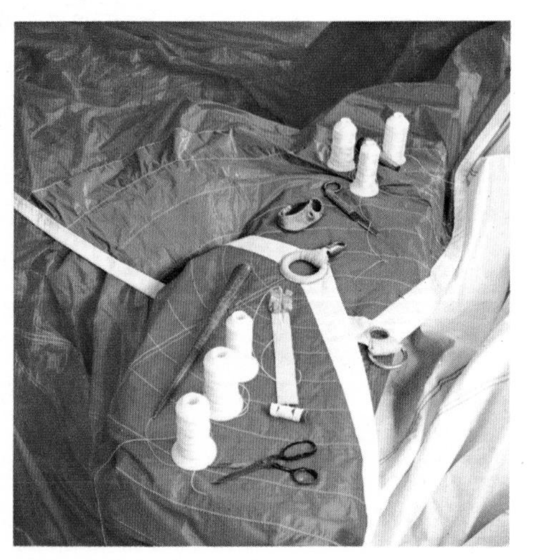

▶ In professional sailmaking, a large area of the loft floor is used to mark out and assemble sails. Sewing and other work is done round the edges of the room.

Sails and sailmaking

Nearly all modern sails are made of synthetic fibre cloths, which hold their shape and do not rot. The old materials of cotton, flax and other natural fibres have almost entirely been replaced.

Sails are made from cloths sewn edge to edge with overlapping seams. The panels are either straight-edged or slightly curved to give shape to the sail. Most sail edges are cut with a slight curve, so the effect of pulling them straight puts a curve in the body sail. Edges are reinforced with sewn-on strips and corners, and other places subject to strain are strengthened with patches. Mainsails are commonly made with the seams at right-angles to the outside edge (leech). A jib may have a main seam which follows the line of pull of the sheet. The cloth seams are then arranged at right-angles to the edges each side of it. This is known as a mitre seam. At one time most sail edges were also roped with three-strand rope sewn on by hand, but such roping is now usually enclosed.

The curve usually given to the leech of a Bermudan mainsail is held to shape by wood or plastic battens. These are seized or sprung into pockets sewn on the sail. The roped edge of a Bermudan mainsail may slide in a grooved mast and boom, and a lanyard tensions the clew along the boom. The head of the sail usually includes a plate to make the leech stand out and the main halliard fastens to this. A mainsail may carry its class insignia with its number if it is registered with the class association. As light shines through most sails, the marks are usually staggered. They are best sewn on, but may be self-adhesive plastic.

PARTS OF A SAIL

1 The curve of the leech is held out by battens in pockets, fixed in several ways. Battens are wood or plastic.

2 Wood or metal masts and spars may have a streamlined shape and be grooved to take the roped edge of the sail. Halliards may pass through the hollow centre.

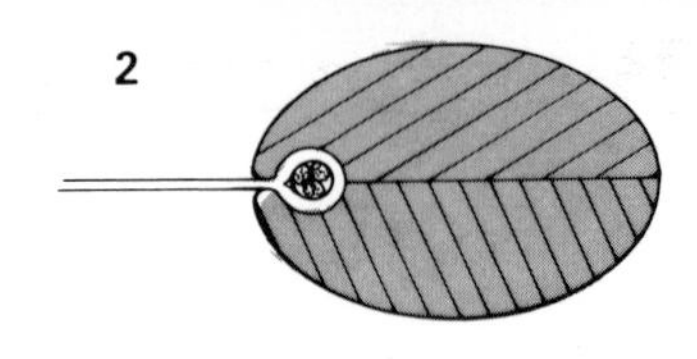

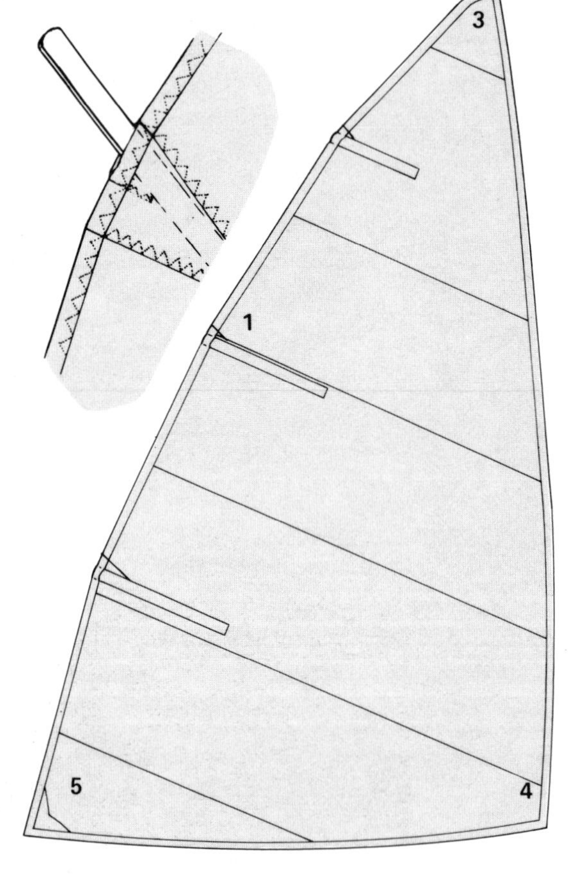

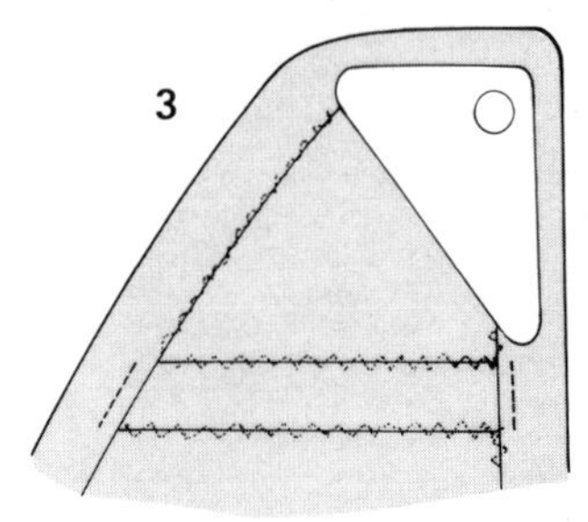

3 The head of the sail may have a metal or wooden plate sewn in to give shape to the top of the sail and hold out the leech to give a greater area of canvas near the top of the sail.

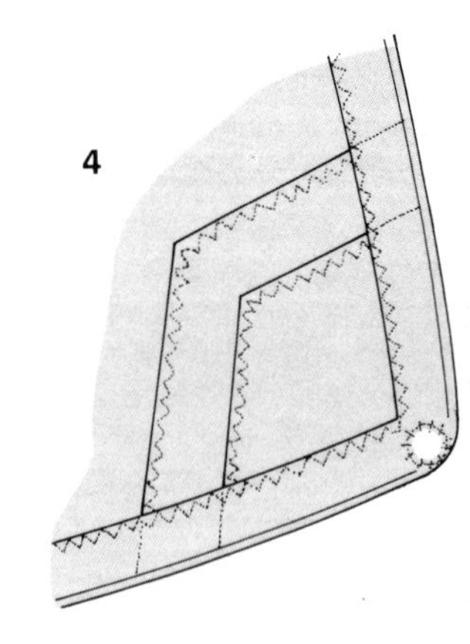

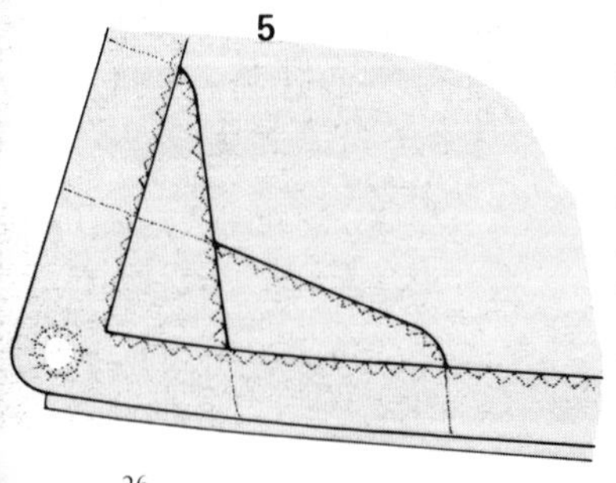

5 The clew corner of the mainsail has reinforcing patches taken along the edges to spread the strain. A lanyard attached to the grommet tensions the foot of the sail. Roping from the foot is carried a short distance up the leech.

4 The edges of a sail are reinforced and the corners are further strengthened by one or more patches that spreads the strain from the grommet or other corner fitting.

Buoyancy and safety

It is important that precautions are taken to ensure, as far as possible, the safety of a boat in an emergency and so prevent sinking. Similarly, it is important that measures to guard against the crew going overboard are put into practice. If somebody does fall in, he should be kept afloat, preferably without effort on his part.

Buoyancy

A wooden boat without much ballast has considerable inherent buoyancy, unlike one made from glass fibre. Consequently a wooden hull needs less reserve buoyancy than a glass fibre one of the same size.

Reserve buoyancy can normally be added to a boat. For smaller craft this can be incorporated without interfering with accommodation, but in larger craft fitting enough to keep a fully waterlogged boat afloat becomes a practical impossibility.

There are several ways of adding reserve buoyancy to a dinghy or half-decked boat. Air in sealed compartments under the foredeck and thwarts or side benches is effective. Alternatively you can use inflatable air bags secured by tapes or straps round the thwarts or to other fixed points.

Air can also be trapped in closed-cell plastic foam. This can be either in the form of blocks secured in place, or injected into cavities in the boat such as the bow of a dinghy.

Racing classes specify how much reserve buoyancy is to be provided and how it is to be placed. For other craft it is important to arrange the buoyancy so the boat floats level fore and aft when it turns on its side, or when it is righted with water inside. More buoyancy at one end than the other can make righting difficult. Another point to watch is the avoidance of excess buoyancy. A capsized boat floating too high because it is over-buoyant may blow away from anyone in the water, and the windage on the exposed hull may make righting difficult.

An open centreboard boat should have its buoyancy disposed so that after it is righted, the top of the centreboard case is above the water level inside. Otherwise water will come in through the case to replace any being bailed.

It is impossible to build in enough reserve buoyancy to take care of a complete

▼ It is important that buoyancy bags or foam are disposed about the boat so it trims level even when capsized.

swamping, if the boat has decking and a cabin with ballast and probably an engine. Instead the decking and cabin top will limit the amount of water getting in. You can also restrict water to the cockpit by making it watertight and blanking off the cabin bulkhead. In craft over about six metres, it is possible to make the cockpit self-draining. However, most shorter cabin craft have the cockpit sole too low for this and water has to be bailed or pumped out.

Crew safety

There is little that can be done in a dinghy to prevent crew falling overboard, although toe straps help. In decked craft there should be grab rails on the cabin top. There may be a pulpit round the bow and guard rails round the side decks to a pushpit aft. In the smallest yacht, these would have to be so low that they would be ineffective. Consequently, it is more usual to provide toe rails to prevent feet sliding.

A safety harness should be worn by anyone moving about the decks of a small yacht. This has a line with a clip, which can be attached to a secure point when going forward in bad conditions.

Clothing should be related to safety. Wet suits have their uses for racing and short periods afloat, but are not suitable for wearing all day. Avoid rubber boots that cannot be easily kicked off. Shoes designed to be non-slip on decks are preferable. Wool is the best material for clothing, as it conserves heat, even when wet. Try not to wear jeans as they become tight and wet in the water so restricting leg movements.

Everyone who goes afloat ought to be able to swim—its importance is obvious particularly for the confidence it gives in

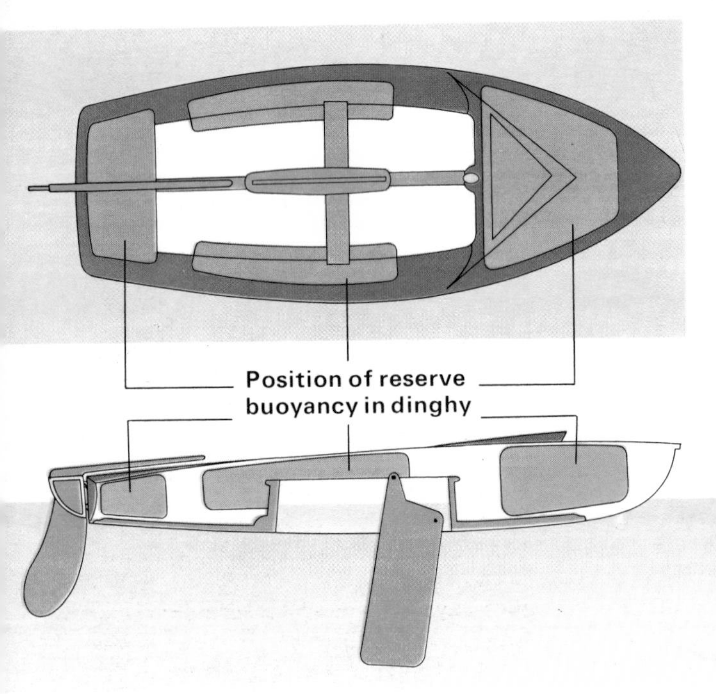

Reserve buoyancy in a dinghy may consist of built-in air compartments, air bags lashed in or blocks of buoyant form, cased or secured in place. It should be disposed so that the boat floats level fore and aft when it capsizes and after it is righted with water in it. The boat should float so the top of its centreboard case is above the water in the righted boat, so bailing can be carried out without more water entering through the case.

▲ Safety on deck is ensured by a safety harness clipped to a strong point.

▶ A lifejacket or buoyancy aid should be regarded as standard wear.

an emergency. However, you do not have to be able to cover long distances. Personal buoyancy should always be worn. It will help to keep you afloat without the need to swim, so you can give your attention to other things, such as righting a dinghy.

The most effective buoyant garment is a lifejacket made to the British Standards Specification. This will turn an insensible person face upwards. If you are knocked out this takes care of you, but some small boat sailors consider the bulk in front a nuisance. An alternative is a buoyancy aid made to the standard of the Ship and Boatbuilders National Federation. This will support its wearer, but he has to be conscious so he can do whatever is necessary to keep the right way up. These buoyancy aids spread the buoyant material, so most are like coats and less bulky to wear.

A lifejacket has buoyant foam mostly in front of the body and around the back of the neck. There is provision for you to blow into it to give extra buoyancy, but the foam buoyancy is sufficient for normal circumstances. There is also a loop in front for a rescuer to use for hauling you out of the water, and a whistle for attracting attention. It is unwise to use older garments that contain kapok or foam linked cells.

A lifebuoy too should be carried for emergency use. This may be a full ring or a U shape made of plastic foam, but older ones are cork. These, and lifejackets, may be fitted with flares or lights to mark their position in the water at night. The helmsman may also sit on a buoyant cushion with roped edges. He then has something to throw immediately, if anyone goes overboard.

Preparing and rigging

The correct arrangement and adjustment of the spars, sails, standing rigging and running rigging are important if the sailing craft is to perform satisfactorily and most efficiently. Preparation before launching or leaving a mooring includes seeing that the mast is properly supported, the various lines of the running rigging are correctly arranged and free to run without obstruction, and the sails are attached ready to be hoisted fully. It is advisable to practise rigging in a sheltered position ashore, as there may be little time to spare for experiment in windy conditions afloat.

The mast

Usually the mast is upright when the boat is afloat. A slight rake aft is preferable to a forward slope and its supporting stays should be sufficiently tensioned to keep it in place. When adjusting lanyards or turnbuckles on shrouds, opposite pairs should be at the same settings. If the shrouds are the same length, this provides a guide to the uprightness of the mast in a crosswise direction.

If the mast is out of the boat, check that the halliards and other attachments are in place and not tangled before mounting it (stepping it). Fix the halliards to their cleats so they cannot be confused with standing rigging when the mast is being positioned.

Arranging the sheets

Check the working of the main sheet because in many small craft it can be arranged in its entirety before the sail is attached to the boom. Where possible have it rove through blocks fastened to a horse or track.

Arrange the two parts of the jib sheet through their leads. The snap shackle or other fitting should be ready to attach to the clew of the sail. Make sure with both sheets that the free ends are coiled clear of obstructions. The ropes must be able to run out without fouling you or any fittings, but put knots in their ends to prevent them slipping back through the leads.

Where to rig a boat

A light dinghy may be rigged ashore and then lifted into

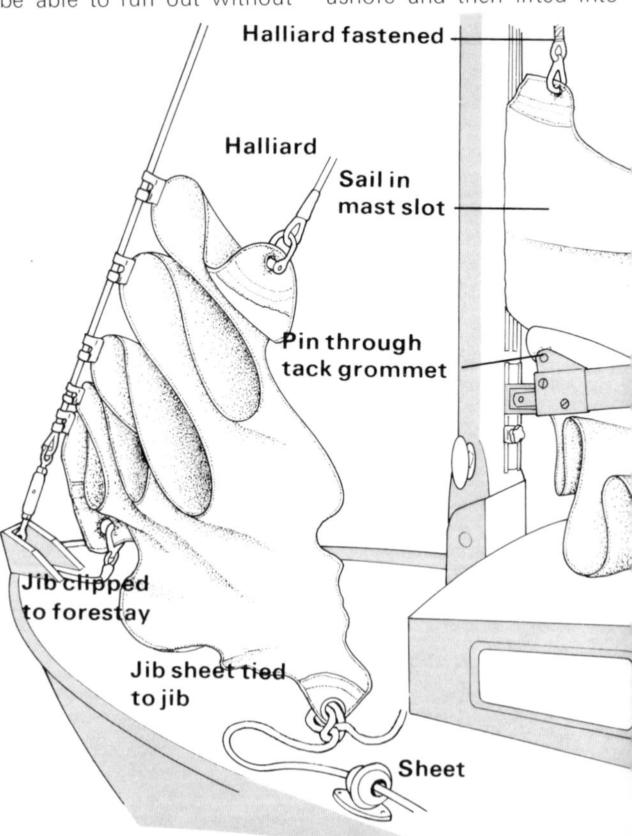

the water ready to sail. Otherwise it is necessary to rig a boat while it is afloat. In both cases remember that what you are hoisting is your source of power. As soon as you raise the sails they will try to function if any wind gets into them. To prevent capsizing or other complications, have the boat head to wind, whether it is ashore or afloat. Do not attempt to restrain a hoisted sail. Let it flap loosely like a flag. Sheets should be allowed to run out as much as necessary — their knotted ends prevent them pulling free.

Hoisting the sails

If the foot of the mainsail slides into a grooved boom, fasten its tack with the pin or lashing. Stretch the sail along the boom using its lanyard, but not so much as to distort the sailcloth. Put all battens in their pockets and make sure they are secure. On some boats the gooseneck is on a sliding track, so fix it temporarily near its upper limit. If there is a topping lift, tension this enough to take the weight of the boom.

Attach the main halliard to the head of the sail and slip the roped edge of the sail into the mast slot. Feed the sail in as it is being hoisted. It may start flapping if there is much wind, so keep yourself clear. With the head fully up, tension the sail by pulling the gooseneck down on its track. If the gooseneck is fixed on the mast, tension by pulling the halliard outwards with one hand while the other takes up the slack round the cleat as the pull is released. When the sail is taking the weight of the boom, slacken the topping lift. If there is a kicking strap, tension this when the gooseneck is in its final position.

After checking that the main sheet is working freely, hoist the jib. Tension its halliard in the same way as the main halliard and secure the surplus rope. In an emergency you may have to cast off the halliards quickly, so it should always be possible to free them without difficulty.

Making fast a halliard

Put several turns round the cleat, then make a half-hitch with the last turn over one arm of the cleat. If the surplus rope has no other stowage, it can be coiled and a part of the coil nearest the cleat taken through the other coils to hitch over the top of the cleat.

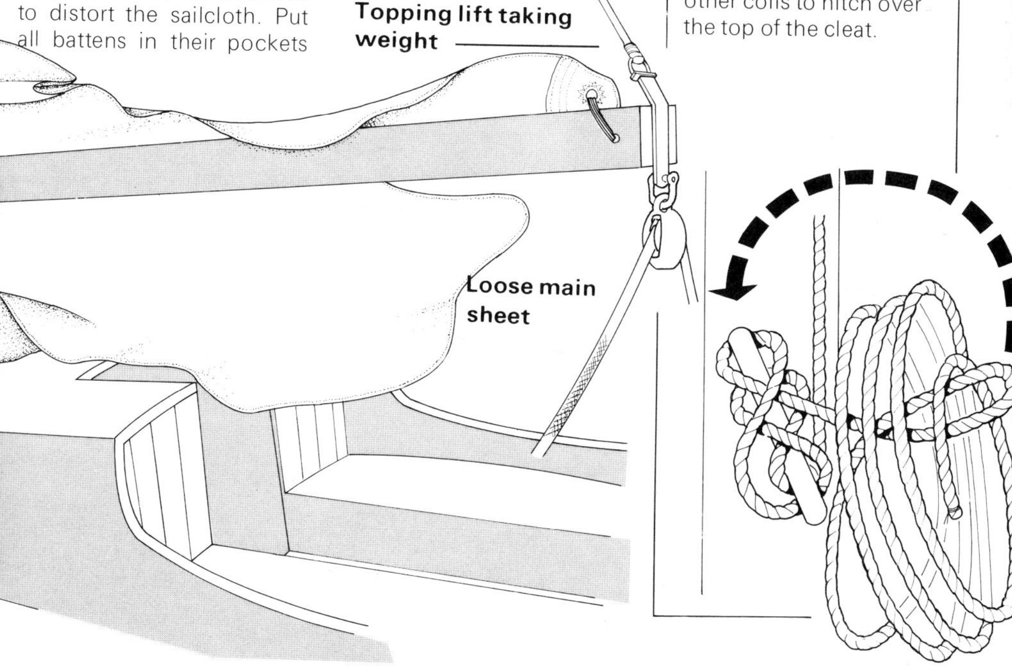

A gunter rig

If the boat has a gunter mainsail, preparation and rigging are similar up to the point where the mainsail has to be hoisted. The sail should be fitted to the gaff while the gaff is on the deck. In most rigs the sail attaches near the gaff jaws. The roped edge of the head is then drawn along the gaff groove and tensioned by hauling a lanyard at its peak. The jaws are engaged with the mast and the halliard attached to the gaff and hoisted as tight to the mast as possible. As the topping lift crosses the sail, slacken it so that it cannot affect the set of the sail.

A lug sail

On boats that have a balanced or standing lug sail and no jib, attach the sail to both spars. If they are grooved, thread the roped edges in and tension from both ends. Where the sail is lashed to one or both spars, tension at the ends with lashings, then use light line to half-hitch through the intermediate grommets and round the spar.

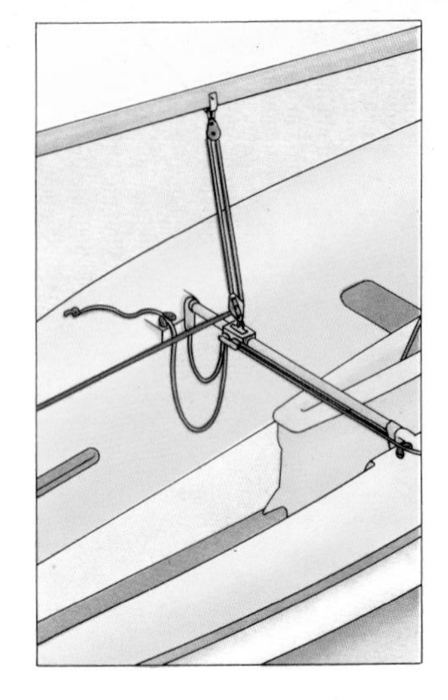

▲ Where a centre main sheet is used, forward of the helmsman, it gives a good set to the sail by pulling the boom down.

▲ Jib sheets are in two parts, brought to fairleads on the gunwales. Only the part on the lee side is used at any one time.

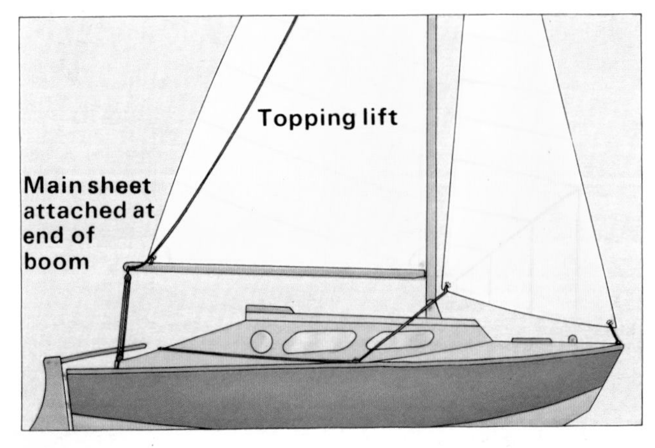

▼ An end arrangement of the main sheet is useful on cruisers because it is out of the way. A topping lift supports the boom when hoisting the mainsail.

The centreboard

See that the centreboard is free to function. If there is a tackle to operate it, note how this works and check that the rope will run freely. It may be necessary to lower the centreboard quickly as soon as the sails start drawing.

The rudder

Mount the rudder, if possible, and fit its tiller, watching that this does not get tangled with the main sheet. If the rudder cannot be fitted until the boat is afloat, have the rudder and tiller ready to slip into place quickly.

▶ With the boat pointing to windward the mainsail is hoisted and tensioned before raising the jib.

Ropework

There are an enormous number of seaman's knots, but those described here should suit most needs. Most modern cordage is synthetic and is smoother than natural fibre ropes, so it may need extra turns to prevent slipping. An unprotected end of synthetic rope will quickly unlay. This can be prevented by melting the filaments with a flame and squeezing them together with moistened fingers. However, a whipping with Terylene or other synthetic thread should be used as well. Most rope is three-stranded, but braided rope is more comfortable to handle and less liable to kink for sheets.

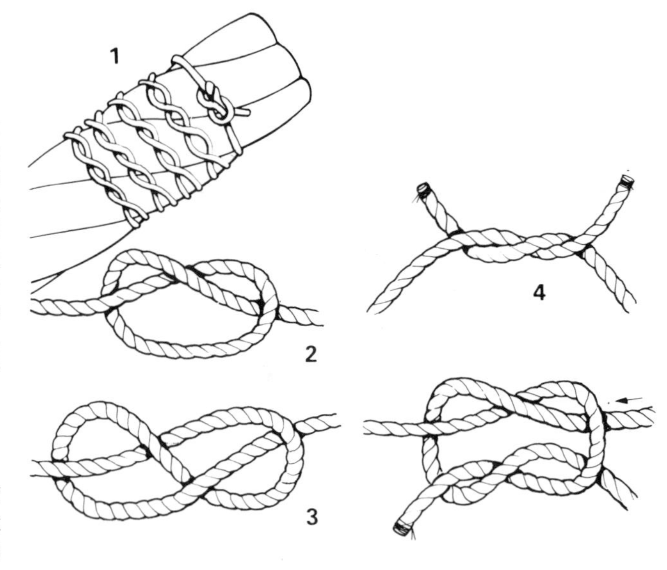

1. West Country whipping

This is an easy whipping suitable for any type of rope. The middle of the line is put behind the rope and the ends brought to the front and twisted together tightly. This is repeated at the back and then alternately front and back until the whipping length is about the same as the diameter of the rope, when the ends are knotted together and cut off.

2. Thumb or overhand knot

Made with a single twist of the rope, this is the simplest stopper knot to prevent a rope's end pulling through your hand or a hole.

3. Figure-of-eight knot

This makes a larger stopper knot. Start as if making a thumb knot, but take the end round the other part and in the other side of the loop.

4. Reef knot

This is one of the best-known joining knots. However, it is only satisfactory if it is bearing against something solid, as it is when tying the points in a traditionally-reefed sail. The two ends are twisted together once and then again the opposite way so that they finish alongside the standing parts. If the ends finish across the knot, it is an unsafe granny. 'Left over right and right over left' is the way many sailors learn the reef knot.

5. Sheet bend and 6. Double sheet bend

The general-purpose joining knot afloat is the sheet bend. One end is doubled back (the thicker if the ropes are different thicknesses) and the other brought up through the loop, round its back and across its front under itself. If there is a considerable difference in the thicknesses of the ropes or they are very wet or greasy, it is better to go round a second time to make a double sheet bend. Most synthetic fibre ropes are slippery enough to justify using the double sheet bend every time. In both sheet bends it is usual for the ends to finish on opposite sides.

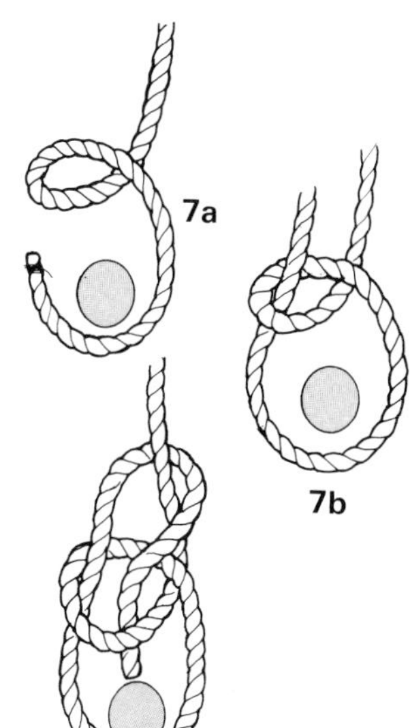

ring, but most are variations on the clove hitch. It may be used as a temporary end fastening, for example when a rope is secured to a bollard in a lock, but for a permanent application there should be a load on both ends. To make a clove hitch, take the end around the spar and over the standing part. Continue the same way round to encircle the spar again and pass the end under its own loop. Bring the two loops close together.

9. Round turn and two half hitches

This is a better fastening for the end of a rope. The standing part is kept taut and the end taken completely round the spar (the round turn). It then goes

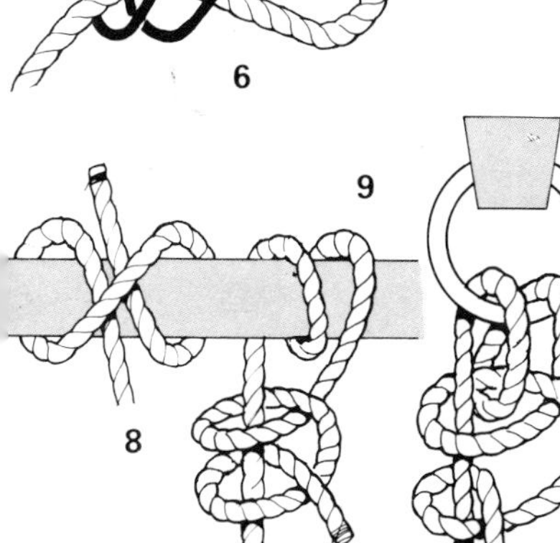

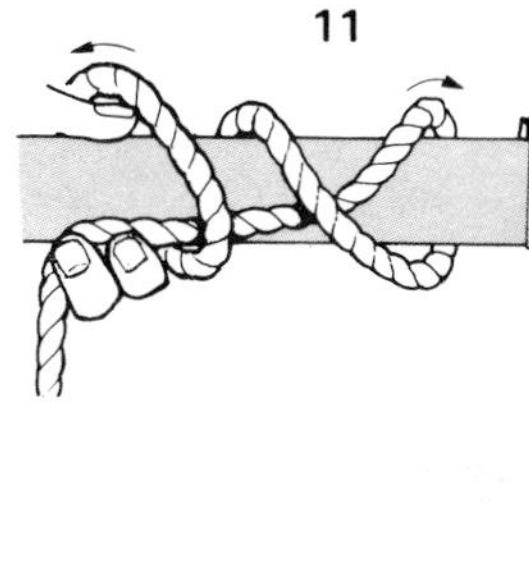

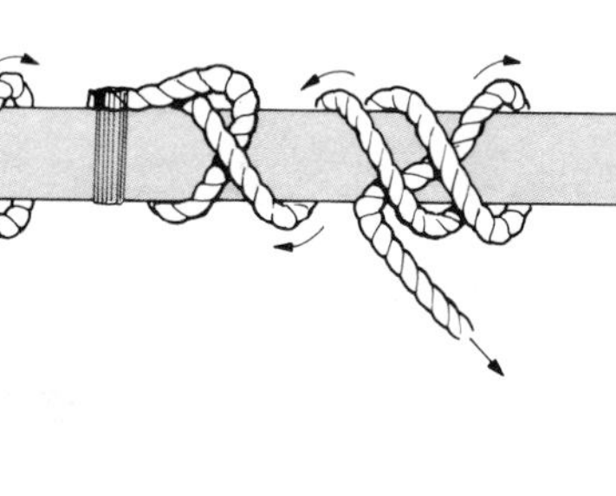

7. Bowline

Of the many knots for putting a loop in the end of a rope, this is the most useful—it holds its shape and is easy to cast off. Enough rope is taken to make the loop, and a small eye formed (7a). The end goes through this (7b), round the standing part, in the direction that pinches the parts of the eye together, and down through the eye to finish between the sides of the loop (7c). Pull the sides of the loop and this end against the standing part to keep the knot in shape.

8. Clove hitch

There are many hitches for attaching rope to a spar or

round the standing part, bringing the end through near the spar, and round again exactly the same to complete the knot. The two half hitches should form a clove hitch round the standing part.

10. Anchor bend

This is the most secure way of attaching a rope cable to

an anchor. It is made like a round turn and two half hitches except that when the first half hitch is made it is taken through the middle of the round turn. However, after it has been under load in water it becomes almost impossible to cast off.

11. Rolling hitch

The primary use of this knot is to attach a rope to a spar. The rope goes twice over the end that is to take the load then round once more behind it and under its own loop. For greatest security the free end is then lashed to the spar.

12. Eye splice

Of the many splices the one most used is an eye in a three-strand rope. Sufficient lengths of end strands are unlaid and their ends sealed by heat. Then the rope is

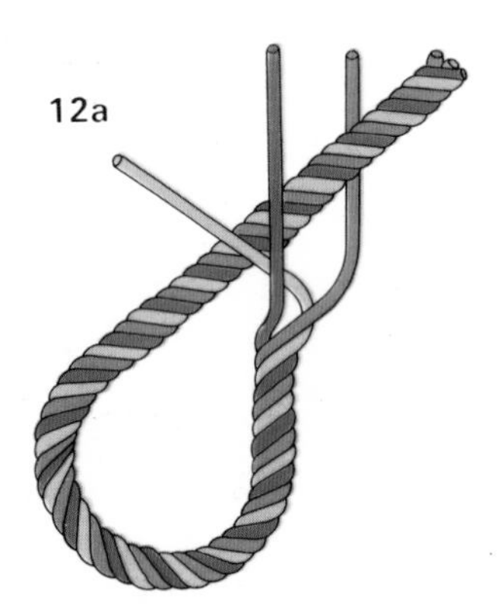

turned back to make an eye of sufficient size, with the ends pointing across the lay of the main part of the rope (12a). Have two ends across the front and let the other go behind. Lift a main strand and tuck the middle one of the end strands under it (12b). Take the end strand nearer the eye under the next main strand (12c).

Turn the splice over and find the main strand that does not have an end under it. Tuck the remaining end there, going the same way

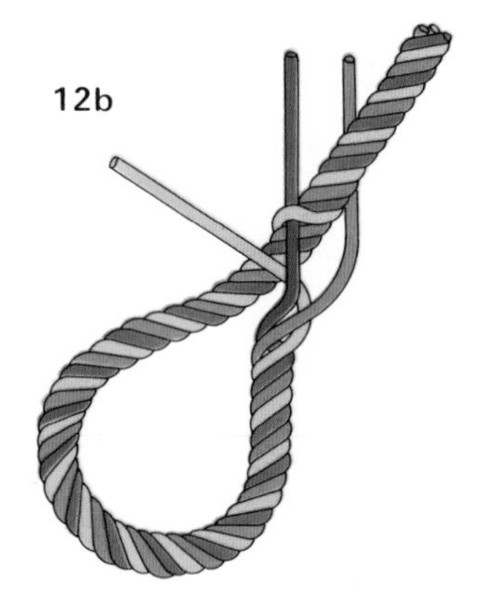

around the rope as the other two ends (12d). Pull the ends tight. There should now be one end projecting from each space in the main rope. Adjust so the ends are in the same plane around the rope and tension is even.

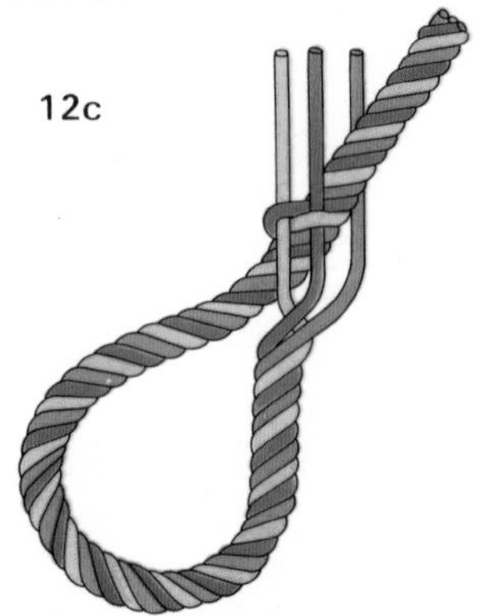

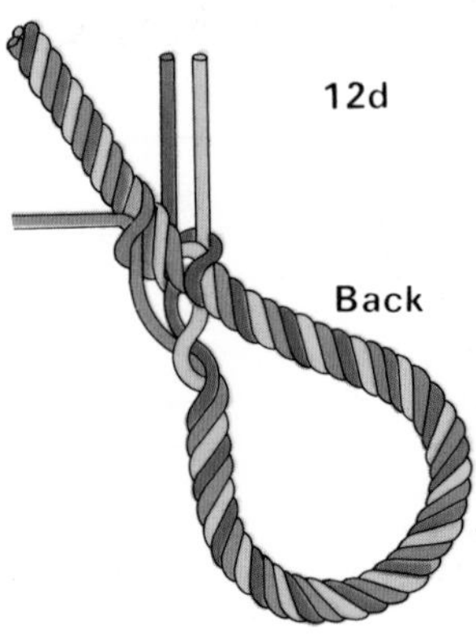

Tuck each end in turn 'over and under one', without letting any end strands cross each other. It is usual to do this three times in natural fibre rope, but in synthetic rope it is better to tuck five times. Some of the fibres may be cut away from each strand for the last tuck so there is a tapered effect (12e). Pull the ends evenly

as they are tucked, but rolling the splice between boards or underfoot on a clean deck will even up the appearance.

Handling a boat

The greatest satisfaction in sailing a dinghy or small cruiser is in being able to make it respond to your wishes. Skill comes with experience and appreciation of what is happening with the wind in the sails and the hull moving through the water. So your reactions should become automatic in the adjustments of sheets and tiller. The following pages give information on a great many sailing situations, which will enable you to go afloat with a basic knowledge of good seamanship.

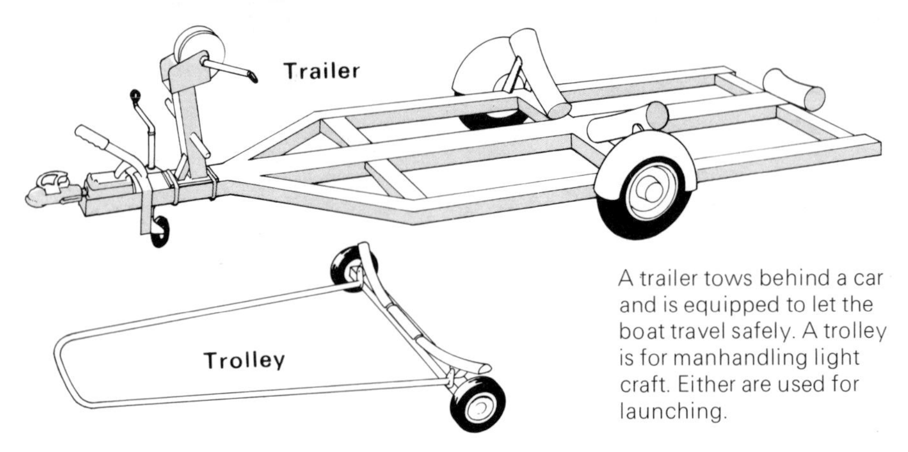

A trailer tows behind a car and is equipped to let the boat travel safely. A trolley is for manhandling light craft. Either are used for launching.

LAUNCHING AND RECOVERY

The techniques of launching and recovery are very similar. A car trailer is usually suitable for all small craft although a trolley may be used for a dinghy.

Launching

Boats are normally loaded onto their trailers with their bows towards the towing end. Consequently, it is most convenient to launch them stern first.

If the wind is light and not blowing directly towards the shore, the sails may be hoisted and prepared before the boat is launched. Otherwise, they may be attached to spars and halliards ready for hoisting, but with the cloth in the boat.

On a hard shore with a moderate slope, the trolley or trailer of a small boat may be manhandled into the water. The towing end is then lifted and this causes the stern to become waterborne allowing the boat to be slid off.

If the boat is heavier or the ramp slopes more steeply, be prepared to restrain the trailer. Some have brakes, so someone should be at the brake lever all the time. Alternatively, it may be better to back the car down with the trailer attached, until the boat can be floated or pushed off. Make sure that the car remains on a sound surface, and use a rope between car and trailer to avoid driving on slippery

▼ A dinghy can be launched by wheeling it far enough into the water for it to float off. Wading is necessary off a beach.

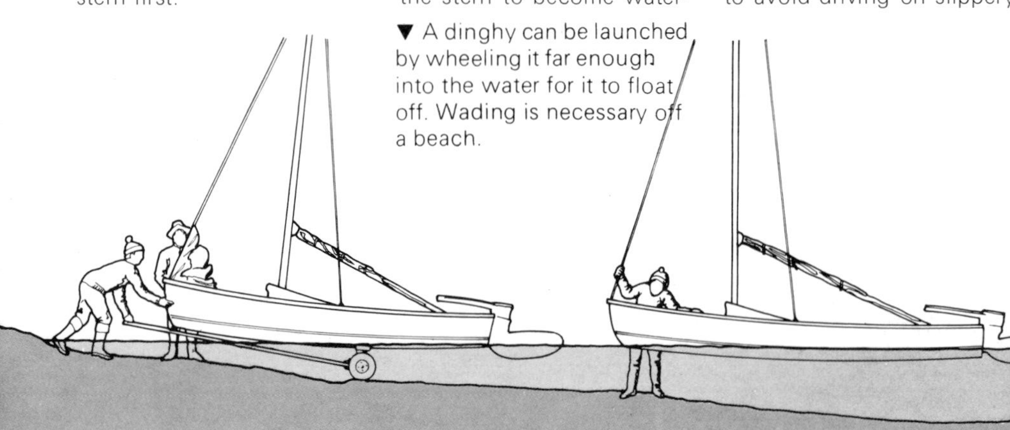

mud. Check how far the ramp goes below the water. A sudden drop might make it difficult to haul back the trailer.

Once the boat is afloat, it may be best to wade alongside to board it, providing it can be easily manhandled. This is necessary on an unsheltered open beach, where it is important to sail out of the shallows quickly.

Launching a large craft usually requires several helpers. The winch cable should remain attached to the bow while the trailer is lowered into the water. It may have to be submerged fairly deeply before the boat can be eased off. The winch cable provides any restraint needed until the boat floats free and it can then be controlled by ropes attached to the bow and stern.

The boat can now be brought alongside and the sails raised if this has not already been done. It may be advisable to sail away under the mainsail only and hoist the jib later.

▲ When launching or recovering a larger trailed craft, have restraining ropes from the stern.

Recovery

Recovering a boat is like launching but in reverse, except there is the problem of lining up the hull with the trailer. It may be possible to jerk the bow onto the end chock. Alternatively, with a light enough boat, it might be possible to position the trailer a short distance under the hull, lever it up and draw the boat on.

Positioning on the trailer becomes easier the further the trailer can be taken into the water under the boat. A winch on the trailer is helpful should the boat be very heavy. If there is much wind or a current across the ramp, use guide ropes taken ashore at a wide angle to keep the hull lined up while it is being drawn up the trailer bed.

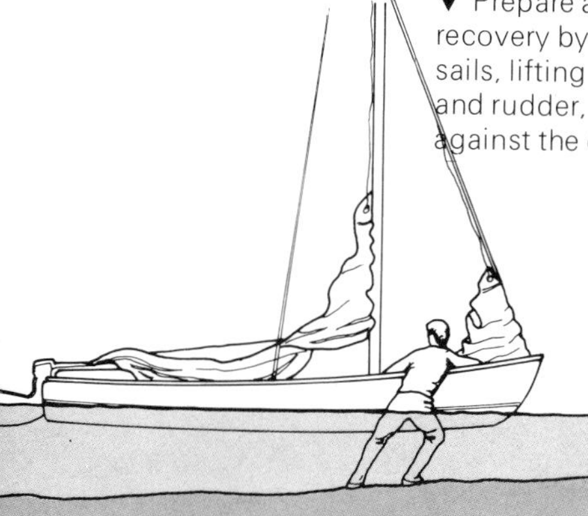

▼ Prepare a boat for recovery by lowering the sails, lifting the centreboard and rudder, and steadying against the current.

▼ Push the trolley in line with the boat and be ready to take its weight.

1 With wind and tide in the same direction parallel to a bank, it is easy to sail away. Push the bow away from the bank and let the jib pull it round before letting the mainsail fill.

2 When the tide is stronger than the wind along the bank, it may be necessary to get away against the tide with the jib and round into the wind. This will enable the mainsail to be hoisted.

3 Getting away with an offshore wind is a matter of letting the boat blow away with the sails slack until there is sufficient room to allow the sheets to be hauled in.

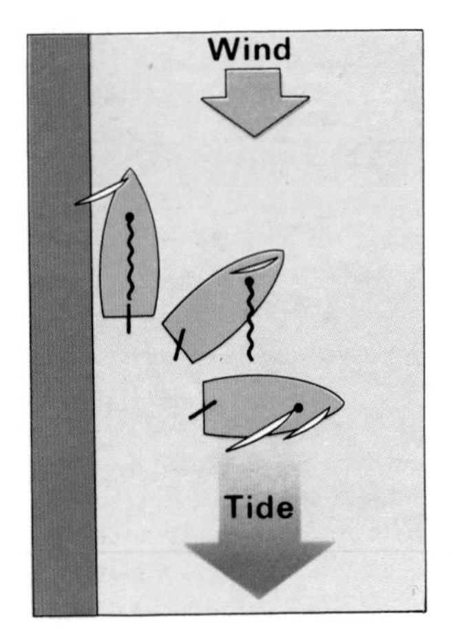

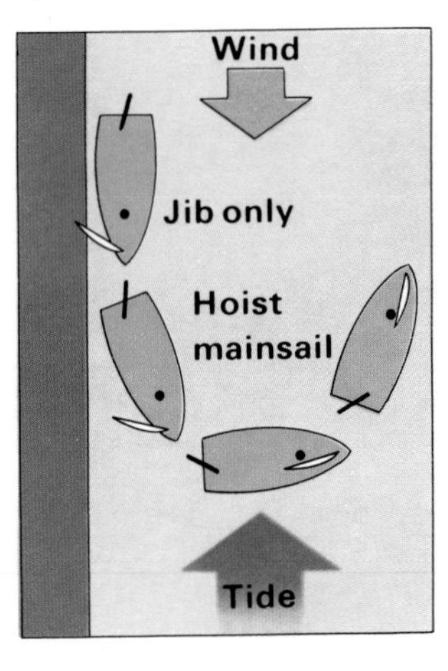

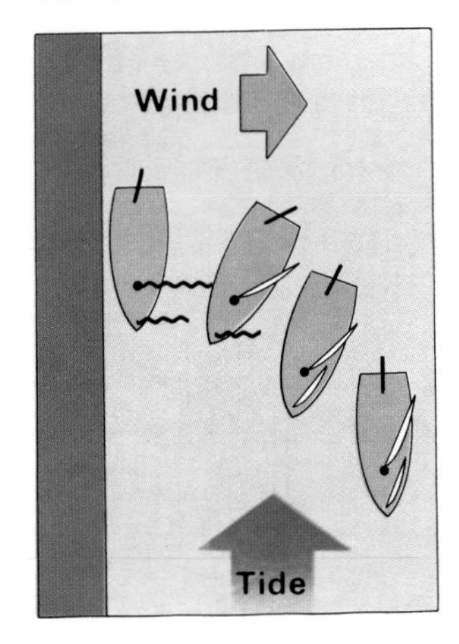

SAILING AWAY

Leaving the shore

Setting off from shore is affected by the direction of the wind in relation to the bank, and the strength and direction of any tide or current.

The simplest conditions are when the wind is blowing along the bank and there is either no stream or it is flowing the same way as the wind (1). The bow of a small boat can be pushed off so the hull is angled towards the wind. The main sheet is hauled in and you can sail away. Instead of pushing off the bow (or in addition to the push), the jib can be 'backed' by being held out the wrong side, so the wind against it pushes the bow over. The stern can be held in until the bow has swung far enough for the mainsail to be set.

If the tide is stronger than the wind, the boat has to be head on to it (2). You may be able to sail off with the jib only hoisted and the mainsail ready in the boat. The rudder can be used to sail across the tide until the boat is turning towards the wind. However, it is not necessary to go fully into it before the mainsail is hoisted.

With the wind blowing offshore, there is little difficulty in getting away (3). Let the hoisted sails flap freely. Then cast off and haul in the mainsail slightly as the boat drifts from the bank. This will give forward motion. As the hull gathers way, haul in and set the jib. Hold the bow to the bank a little longer than the stern, so the hull is at an angle to the wind as the main sheet is pulled in. It may be possible to haul in the main sheet while the boat is still held to the bank, particularly if the tide is strong. Pressure from the water and sail will cause the bow to turn away from the bank and speed is gained quickly.

If the wind is blowing onto the shore (4), getting away is more difficult. It might even be impossible under sail alone. Providing the bank is low and the boom will clear it, the sails can be allowed to flap downwind over the bank. If the bank is high, you will not be able to get away with the sails hoisted and the boat must be rowed or driven off with a motor. Then it can be turned into the wind and the mainsail hoisted first.

From a low lee shore the important thing is to get the bow away at an angle to the wind and the bank. This allows the mainsail to be brought to a close-hauled position and the boat can start sailing quickly before it is driven back on to the bank. Current against the bow helps.

Leaving a buoy

When the boat is moored to a buoy, you are able to assess the relative strengths of the tide and wind from the angle the boat takes up (5). A light boat sits on the surface and is mainly affected by the wind. But if it has a keel or the centreboard is lowered, the boat angle will be the result of these two forces. If the wind is still stronger than the tide, the boat will be towards the wind. The sails can be hoisted, the boat got ready, and the mooring slipped so you sail away easily.

With a strong tide and little wind the boat may be swung across the wind (6). If the tide swings the boat stern to wind, it is inadvisable to sail. Under such conditions it is unlikely that the boat could be sailed well enough to make headway against the tide. With the centreboard up, the boat should take up an attitude more head to wind. Sails can be hoisted and the boat sailed away, with the centreboard lowered as soon as you are moving.

Leaving a shallow shore

A further complication comes in getting away from shallow water. A dinghy cannot be properly controlled until its centreboard is down preventing leeway. A member of the crew gets wet as he pushes the boat out of the shallow water, preferably keeping it as near head-to-wind as possible, then he climbs on board as the boat begins to sail. If the wind is along or off the shore this will help. However, with a strong onshore wind it may be necessary to get away from the shore by other means, and then hoist sail.

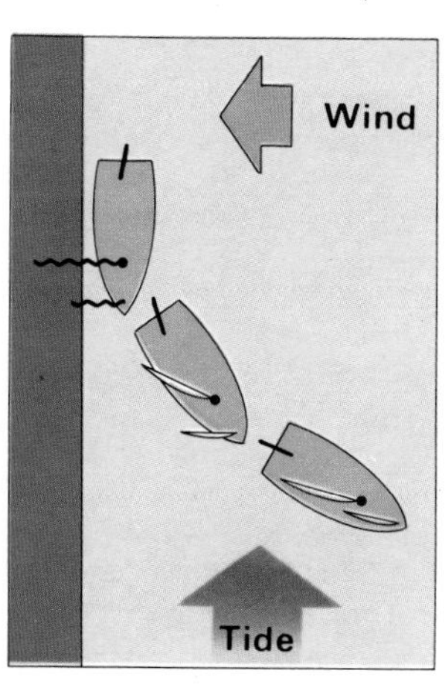

4 With an onshore wind, it is not always possible to sail away. However, it may be possible to push the bow round into the wind. The sheets can be pulled in and the boat can sail away close-hauled.

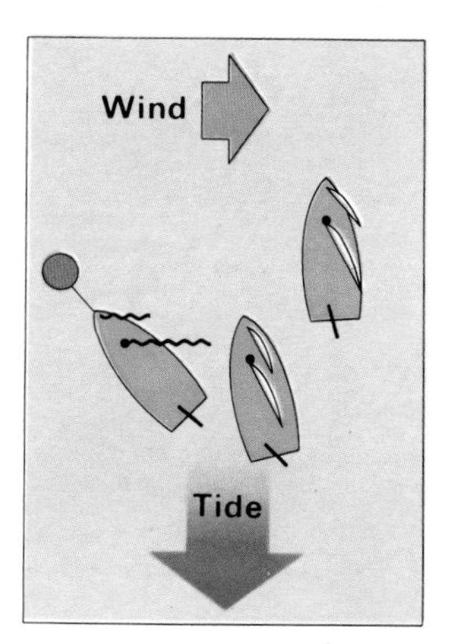

5 When moored to a buoy, the position a boat takes up reflects the relative strength of wind and tide. It can be sailed away if its stern is away from the wind, indicating a breeze stronger than the current.

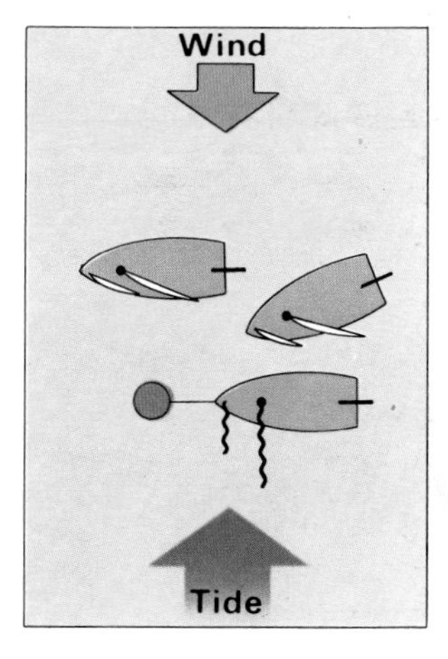

6 If the strength of the tide forces the boat stern to wind when it is moored to a buoy, the boat is sailed away with its centreboard up until it can be turned into wind. The centreboard is then lowered.

SAILING IN MANY DIRECTIONS

The skill in sailing involves using the wind to make the boat go in the direction you want. This is achieved by setting the sails at the correct angles. But remember, you cannot sail closer than about 45° to the wind.

Reaching

The easiest direction to sail in is at right-angles to the wind. This is called reaching. Turn the boat so the wind is abeam. Then haul in the sheet until the end of the boom is just outside the transom and the average angle of the sail is about 45° to the boat. You should have little need to move the tiller as you sit on the windward side. If there is a jib, this should be set to the same angle as the mainsail.

When in a dinghy, it is important for you and the crew (if there is one) to be correctly placed. You can tell when you are in the right position when you need to pull the tiller a little towards you to maintain course. This is called a 'weather helm' and is a safety precaution. In an emergency, if you released the tiller, it would swing to the centre and the boat would turn into the wind and stop. If it had to be pushed away to hold a course—a 'lee helm'—, releasing it would allow the boat to turn off the wind and go on sailing, possibly leaving you in the water and unable to catch up. In a light boat, moving bodies forward would increase a weather helm.

Changing course

Having reached as far as you want to go, you turn round to go back by 'going about'. This is the manoeuvre used to turn a boat with its bow towards the wind. You tell your crew, 'ready about' or 'lee-o', and push the tiller away from the wind. The boat will start turning into the wind and your mate releases the jib sheets and gets ready to change sides. As the boat gets directly into the wind with the sails flapping, you change sides and change hands on the tiller and sheet, ready to reach back on your course. The boom crosses over and the sail fills, with no need for sheet adjustment if both ways are exactly at right-angles to the wind. Your crew hauls in the jib sheet to set the sail at about the same angle to the wind as the mainsail.

Sailing a course

Luffing and close-hauling

By hauling in the sail more tightly than you do for reaching, the boat will turn closer into the wind—'luff'. You should adjust course with the rudder so the sail remains full, without any tendency to flap. When the boom is hauled in tightly and the boat is sailing as close to the wind as it can, you are then 'close hauled' and sailing on a 'board' to windward.

Tacking

If your destination is more directly to windward, the only way you can get there

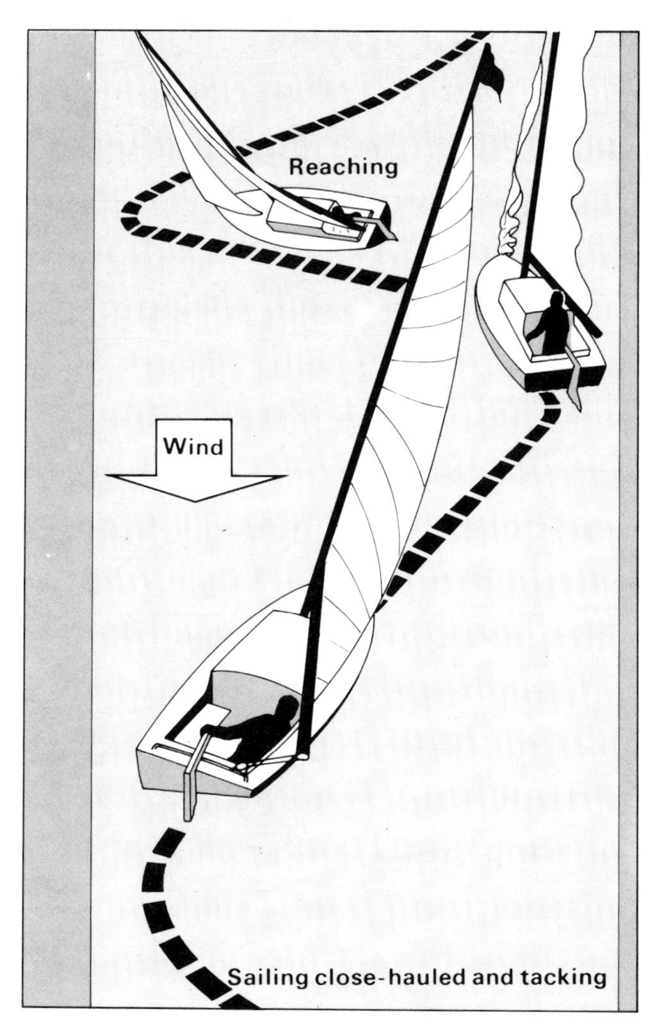

is to 'tack'. This entails sailing a zig-zag course at alternate close angles to the wind. But you may make long and short boards if your destination is not directly upwind or you are in the confines of a narrow of twisting channel diagonal to the wind direction.

You have to go about at the end of each tack. Do not push the rudder over fast or too far. It is not very effective at more than about 45° to the centreline of the boat. If it is pushed much further it acts as a brake and ceases to steer effectively. The boat should continue through the water while turning on an easy curve. The boat must have enough speed to take it through the 'eye' of the wind so the sails fill on the other tack. If you judge that there is not sufficient momentum to carry you round, it is possible to gain speed by going slightly less close to the wind before tacking. However, you will lose some progress to windward. If you are unsuccessful and stop facing into the wind, the boat is 'in irons'. You can get out of this without paddling by 'backing the jib'. Hold it out towards the outside of the turn and the wind may push the bow round far enough for the mainsail to fill.

It may be impossible to build up enough speed to tack by sailing as close-hauled as possible. This is particularly so with a large boat in a narrow channel and the wind ahead. It is better then to concentrate on speed

▼ In a ballasted boat, a better view ahead and of the sails is from the lee side.

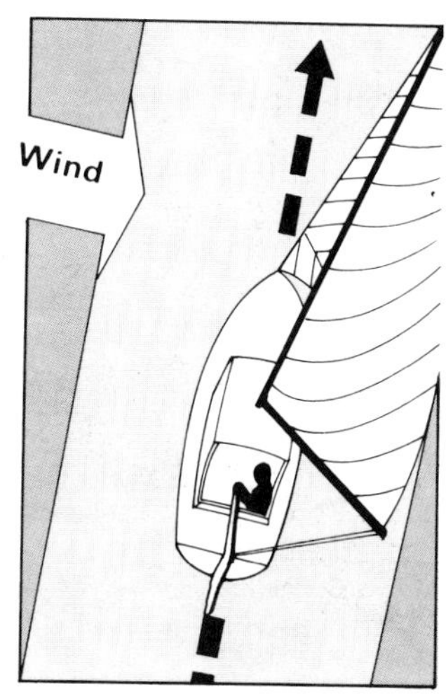

by sailing nearer a reaching course each way. Go about slowly gaining as much progress as possible.

Running

Sailing away from the wind is called 'running'. The mainsail should be set at right-angles to the boat if the wind is directly from behind. However, there is a risk that the wind may change slightly and a gust get behind it. This will cause the sail to cross suddenly to the other side—gybe. Trim the boat immediately otherwise there could be a capsize, or someone may be hurt by the flying boom. A controlled gybe, however, is acceptable in some circumstances.

It is often better not to sail directly downwind, but to steer a course that brings the wind slightly to one side, opposite to that on which the boom is.

When sailing with the wind directly behind, the jib may be screened by the mainsail and so is ineffective. This can be rectified by 'goose-winging' it—holding it out by hand or a spar on the opposite side to the mainsail.

▶ Rounding a buoy by going about. As the boom swings across, the crew moves to his new position before the helmsman so the boat remains balanced. The boat will then need to be trimmed for the new tack.

Wearing

When following a downwind course on a winding river, it might be necessary to change the boom from one side to the other.

In a strong wind, the safest way of doing this is by 'wearing'. Instead of turning the boat to follow the river and cause a gybe, the helm is put the other way and a tight circle is followed.

Running

Gybing

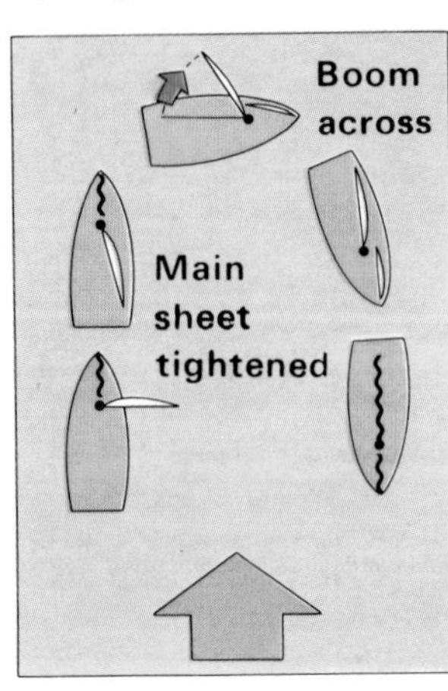

Wearing

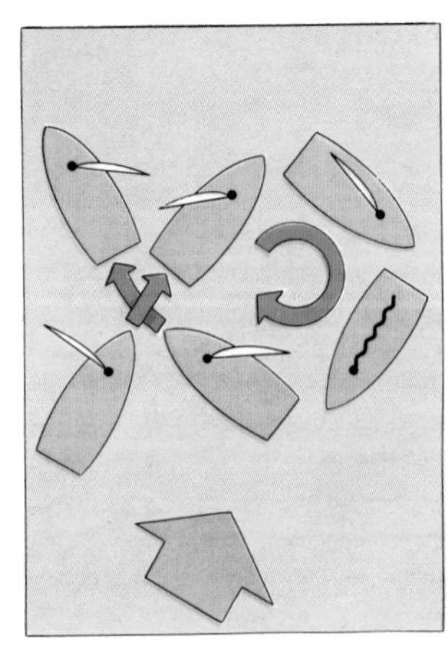

This swings the bow up into the wind and the boom crosses over as it does when going about on a tack. The mainsail is empty of air until it fills on the other side.

Reducing speed and stopping

A sailing boat has no brakes. To slow it down, the sheets are eased so some of the wind is spilled from the sails. Without altering course this makes the sails less effective and therefore reduces the speed.

The only way to stop a boat under sail is to turn its bow directly into the wind. Without any driving power, the sails will flap like flags.

Attempting to slow or stop the boat when the wind is aft is more difficult. It may be possible to let the jib fly or lower it, but the mainsail will continue to draw whatever is done with its sheet. Consequently it is best to try and foresee any need to stop and make sure you have room to turn into the wind. Lowering sails that are drawing, as a means of stopping, is undignified and dangerous.

COMPLETING A COURSE

Having sailed to your destination you then have to come alongside, pick up a buoy, or anchor. Preferably do this under sail. The final approach should always be upwind, wherever possible, so you can spill air from the sails and stop the boat.

1 The approach to a landing stage when the wind is along the bank is on a reach. Then turn the boat towards the wind with the sheets eased, so the sails are flapping when you make your arrival.

2 An upwind landing stage can be approached from one side sailing close-hauled. When nearly there, the boat is turned onto a reach and the jib and then the main sheets eased.

3 If there is room for the boom to extend over a downwind landing stage, sail in from one side. Then lower the jib and sail onto a reach with a progressively eased main sheet as you approach the bank.

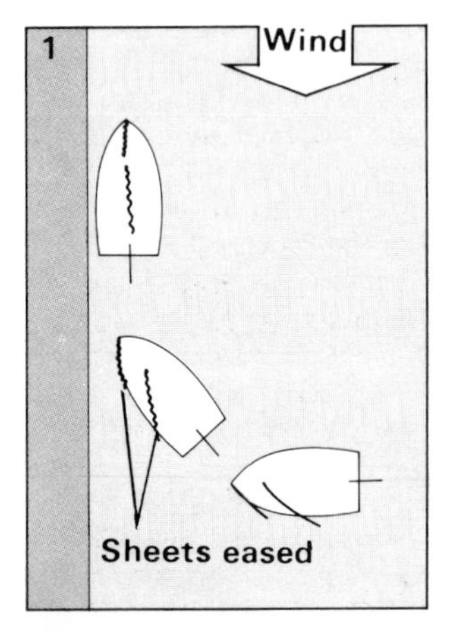

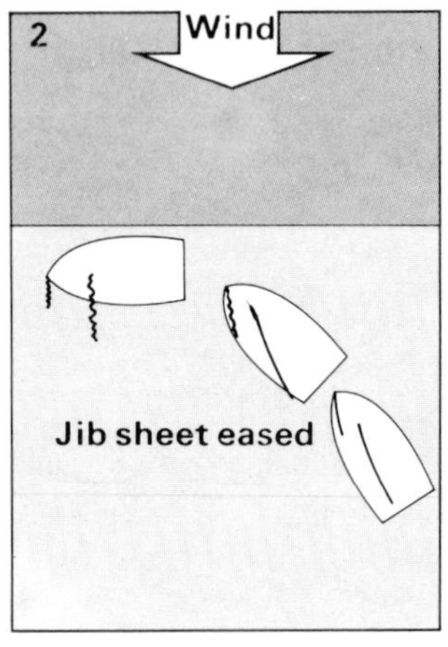

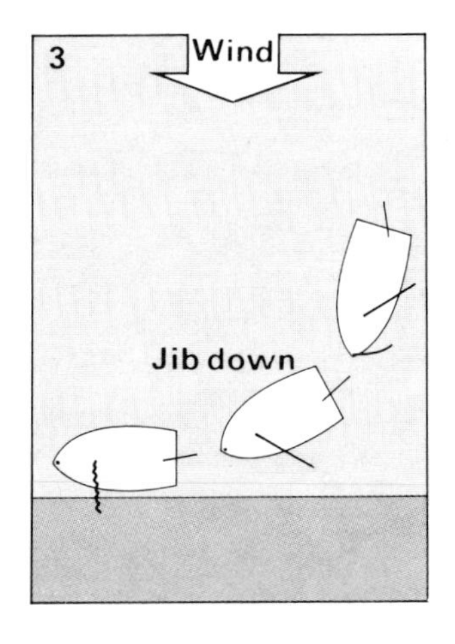

Approaching a bank

The easiest approach is to a landing stage to which you can reach, turn into the wind and finish with the sails flapping (1). It may be advisable to drop the jib and come in under the mainsail.

It is almost as easy to come alongside when the wind is blowing off the bank. You approach on a curving course. The jib is eased or lowered and you ease the main sheet as you come alongside (2). Keep sailing to the last and hold the bank to prevent being blown off again.

Approaching a landing stage downwind (3) is more difficult as you have less control. In a strong wind, it may be impossible under sail without crashing against the bank. In a light wind, sail to one side of the stage, so you reach in with slackened sheets.

Where the boom will not clear a downwind bank, or the wind is strong, turn into the wind and quickly lower the mainsail (4). Backing the jib briefly will push the bow round, and you sail in under the jib alone. You can even get in completely in reverse with a backed jib (5). In both cases rudder handling is important. If the onshore wind is strong, it may be better to drop all sails and paddle in.

Picking up a buoy

If you want to pick up a buoy in still water, aim for a point slightly to one side of downwind. Then sail on a curving course (6), so you arrive into wind with just enough speed for your mate to grab the buoy over the bow. Make sure the buoy is kept at the bow, or the wind will turn the boat and fill the sails. Should this occur, the only safe thing to do is sail away and approach again.

Water movements can complicate these procedures. Coming in against the stream under sail when the stream is stronger than the wind makes it difficult to lower the sails. It may be wiser to turn into the wind before getting there and lower one or both sails, finally getting in under oars or motor.

surf, preferably stern first, with the aid of oars or paddles. And go over the side before the boat grounds.

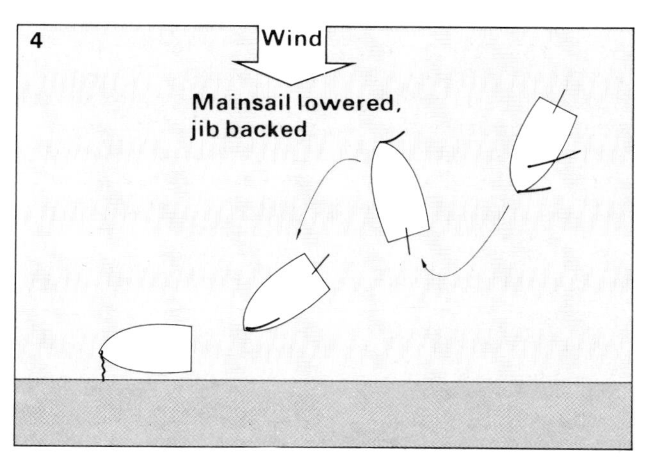

4 Where the downwind bank is high, approach it by first rounding into the wind to lower the mainsail. Then back the jib to turn back towards the bank and sail in using the jib.

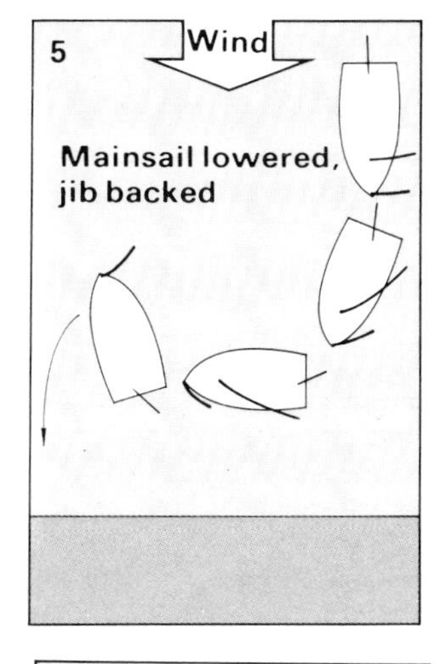

5 It may only be possible to arrive at a downwind destination backwards after lowering the mainsail.

Approaching a shallow beach

Coming into a shallow beach may not be difficult if the wind is off or along the shore. Sail in diagonally to the wind. Then when it is so shallow that the centreboard has to be raised, lower the mainsail. You might even find it possible to get in using the jib alone. If the wind is onshore, a neat landing may be impossible. Turn the boat upwind and lower the sails. Allow the boat to drift through the surf, preferably stern first, with the aid of oars or paddles. And go over the side before the boat grounds.

Anchoring a boat

The anchor cable (usually rope) should be at least three times the depth of water. Make the end fast. Bring the boat into the wind at the point where the anchor is to be lowered. When the boat is virtually stationary, lower the anchor over the bow.

It may be better to lower the jib before coming up to anchor. If the wind and tide are from different directions, lower, or partly lower, the mainsail. The boat will drift astern under the effect of the wind or tide, or both. When cable equal to at least three times the depth of water has run out, make it fast to the bollard. If there is much tidal range, work on three times the greatest depth.

6 Sail up to a buoy on a curved course from either side and finish head to wind.

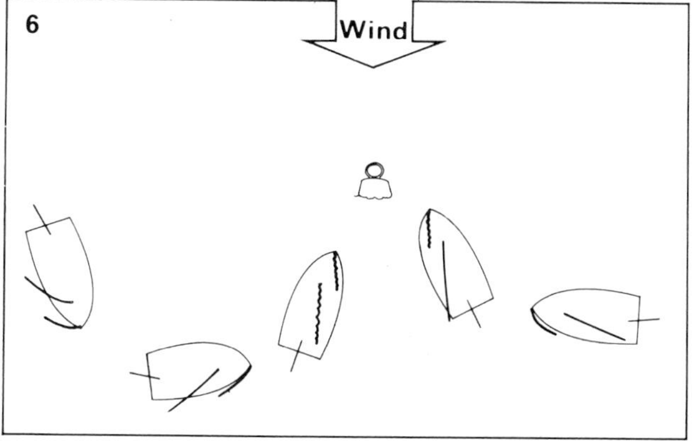

Better boat handling

Although you can soon learn the basics of sailing, it is always possible to improve your skills. You never reach a stage where you can say you know all about it. Your sailing will improve as you get to know your boat and its equipment. As you gain in skill, there are several variations in technique that help in getting a better sailing performance. After that it is largely a matter of learning by experience —your own and that gained by watching and sailing with other people.

Position of the hull in the water

A boat is designed to sail best with the hull upright. It may be exciting to sail with the lee gunwale almost under, but the speed is likely to be more if the hull is trimmed nearer vertical. The speed also increases if as much of the hull length as possible is in the water. The hull should be slightly down at the stern rather than at the bow. But do not have the stern so low that much of the transom goes below the waterline, as this causes excessive drag. This fore and aft trim is best noted by an observer away from the boat. Adjustments can then be made by repositioning yourself and your mate. The correct placing is important particularly in smaller craft.

Role of the crew

In a small boat, transverse trim is carried out mainly by moving the weight of those on board. Therefore, one of the main functions of the second person, or 'crew', in a dinghy is to act as portable ballast. He should position himself accordingly. This often means moving before the helmsman after a change of direction, as the helmsman may still be adjusting the main sheet. Quick and understanding action by the crew can make an appreciable difference when sailing in a way that involves frequent course changes.

Besides moving within the boat it is frequently necessary to get more leverage with the weight available by sitting out as far as possible. Many small boats have toe straps each side of the centre of the boat which aid this procedure. After going about the crew should be holding the jib sheet from the lee side, although not necessarily hauling it in immediately. He should have his feet under the toe strap ready to move his weight outwards as necessary to trim the boat. If the helmsman is ready quickly with his sheet and tiller, he also gets his feet under the strap. He is then ready to

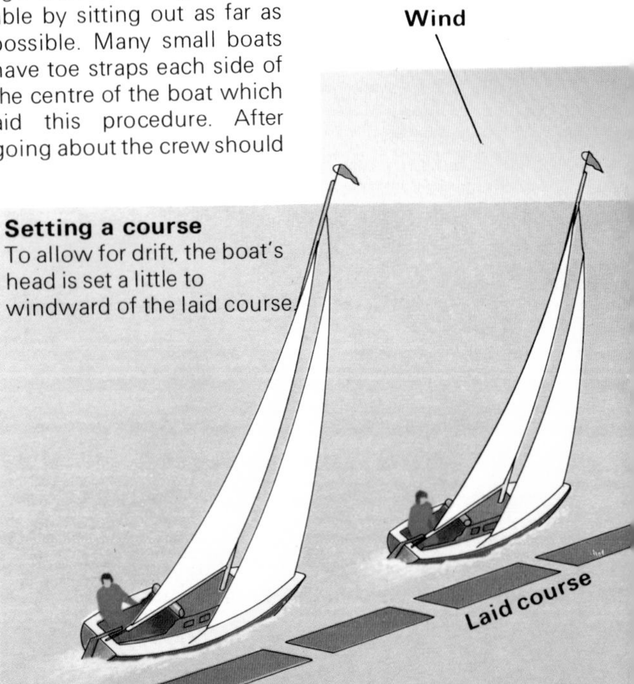

Setting a course
To allow for drift, the boat's head is set a little to windward of the laid course.

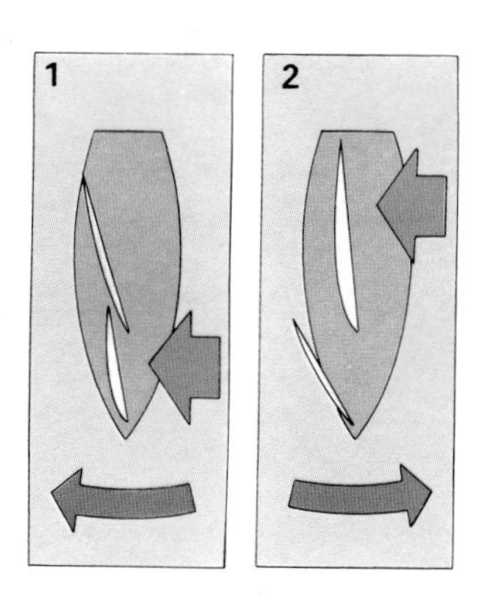

With the jib hauled in tighter than the mainsail (1), there is a tendency to turn off the wind. If the mainsail is tighter (2), the boat tries to turn to windward. When going ahead (3), the boat turns the opposite way to the direction in which the tiller is pushed. And when going astern (4), the rudder effect is reversed.

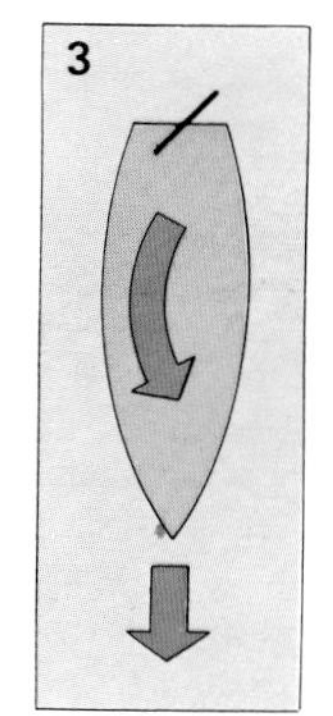

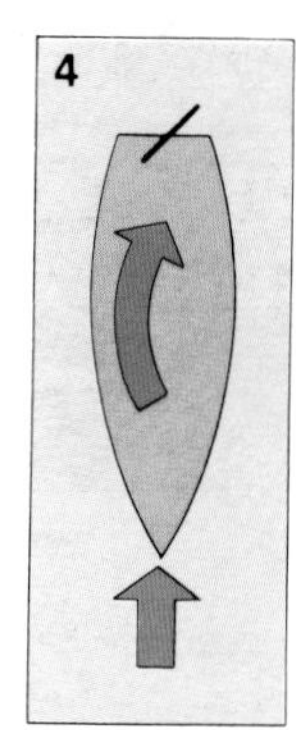

add his weight if necessary as he hauls in the sail. When tacking to windward the mainsail should be hardened before the jib.

As boats get larger, fixed ballast concentrated on the keel reduces the importance of crew weight. However, in some small cabin boats a large number of passengers concentrated aft in a cockpit can affect the trim of a boat enough to reduce its sailing efficiency.

Many helmsmen prefer to steer from the lee side of the cockpit if crew positions do not affect the trim. This gives them a better view forward and they can more easily observe the set of the sails. They can see the first signs of shaking or flapping if the sails are brought too close to the wind. Other members of the crew may then help with trim by sitting to windward.

Use of the centreboard

The sole purpose of an unweighted centreboard or daggerboard is to limit leeway. It is aided in this if the boat is sailed as near up-

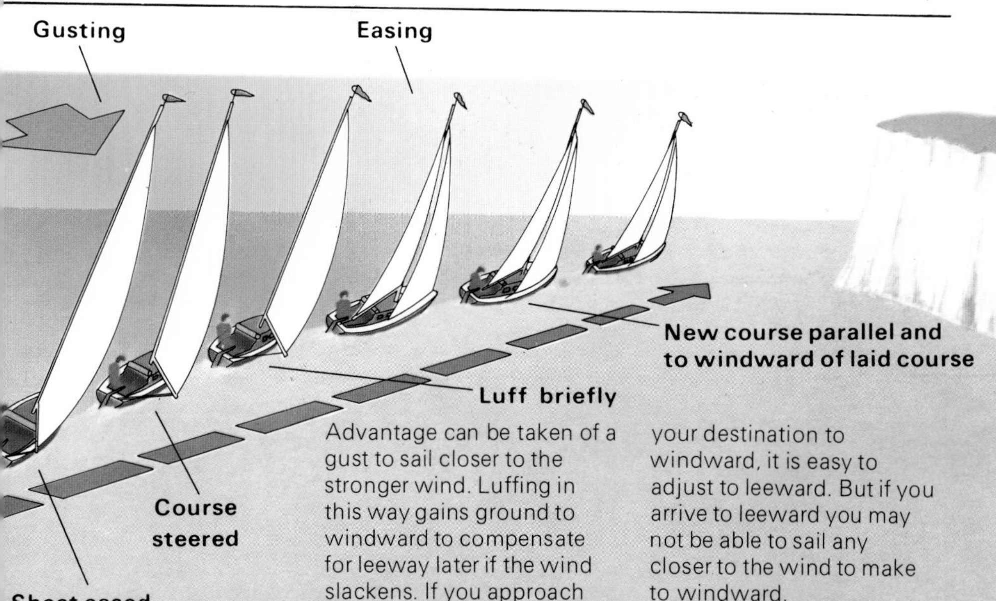

Advantage can be taken of a gust to sail closer to the stronger wind. Luffing in this way gains ground to windward to compensate for leeway later if the wind slackens. If you approach your destination to windward, it is easy to adjust to leeward. But if you arrive to leeward you may not be able to sail any closer to the wind to make to windward.

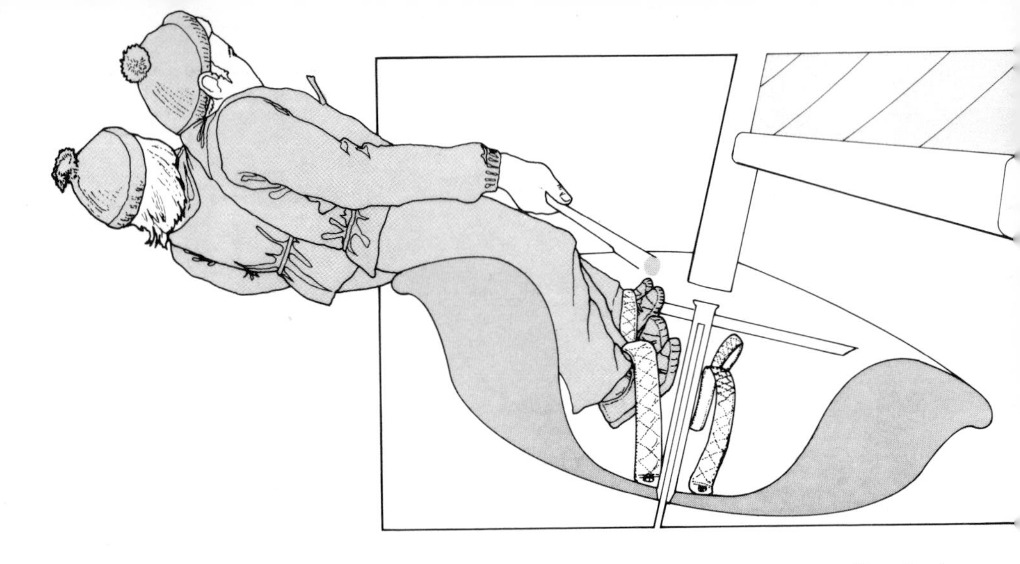

▲ Toe straps allow body weight to be placed further out to balance the effect of heavy wind on the sails.

right as possible. It does not have any effect on stability or trim.

Without the centreboard down, a hull will make considerable leeway when attempting to sail with the wind in any direction except within a few degrees of right aft. Drag is therefore reduced if the centreboard is raised for running before the wind. For all other directions of sailing it is usually fully down.

A weighted centreboard contributes to stability as well as to the reduction of leeway. It is probably best kept fully down at all times when the water is deep enough. It may help to partially raise it when running.

Dealing with leeway

Leeway cannot be avoided and is more apparent when sailing some distance. If a course is set for a distant point, you will actually need to aim to windward of it, so allowing for leeway. You can judge what allowance to make as you get to know your boat. In a strong steady wind there may be less leeway than in a light and variable one. A boat sailed fast tends to make less leeway than when it is only moving slowly.

Use of the rudder

The rudder should be trailing almost directly astern when a boat is sailing correctly on course. This causes minimum drag. A slight weather helm (tiller to windward) for extra safety is also acceptable. But if you find that you have to hold the tiller some way from straight to keep the course you want, there is something wrong. Look astern at the flurry of water to see the extra drag that is being caused. You may have the boat badly trimmed or you may have the sails set wrongly. Try moving the crew or ballast, or adjust your sheets—one sail may be at a very different angle from the other.

The underwater part of a rudder assists the centreboard and the hull in resisting leeway. Make sure that the blade of a lifting rudder is fully down at most times. The only time it may help to raise it partly to reduce drag is when running.

Setting the sails

Under most circumstances, the average angles of the mainsail and jib are kept about the same. On a normal course this will give the best results. Alternatively, they can be manipulated in relation to each other to control the direction of the boat or to help maintain course without excessive use of rudder. Hardening the jib

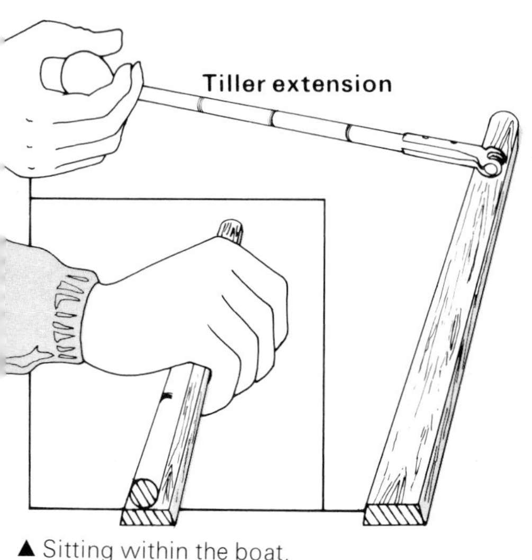

▲ Sitting within the boat, the helmsman's hand is directly on the tiller, but he swings out an extension when sitting-out.

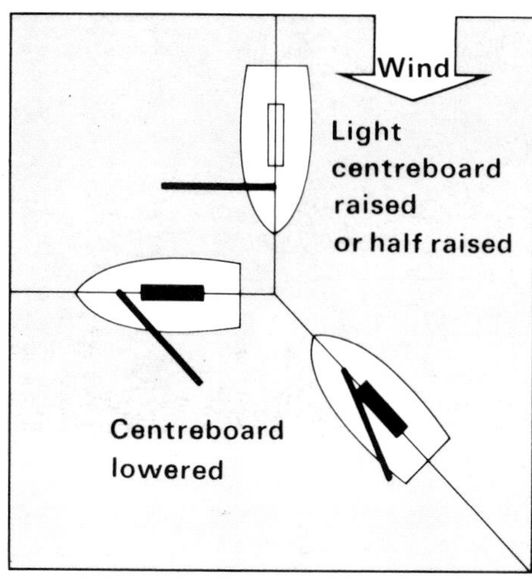

▲ On most courses the centreboard is down to reduce leeway, although it can be raised when running to reduce drag.

much more than the mainsail when the wind is abeam or forward of it, tends to push the bow off the wind. If the mainsail is hardened and the jib loosened or lowered, there is a tendency for the boat to turn towards the wind. Variations between the settings of the two sails can be felt through the tiller. A helmsman should learn to be sensitive to its feel and so be able to judge whether any sheets ought to be trimmed.

The relation of the two sail angles needs to be understood when tacking and going about to windward. A hull that turns easily and carries enough way may go about whatever is done to the sails. Some hulls do not turn easily, and in light airs any hull may need careful handling of the sails if it is to go about at all.

For the most successful turn under difficult circumstances, 'ready about' is called, the jib sheet is eased and the main sheet hauled in as the tiller is pushed slowly to leeward. The mainsail then has a weathercock effect to help turn the boat. Neither you nor your crew should move suddenly across the boat, remain central while it turns directly upwind. The sails will empty and flap, but the tiller is held on the turn. As the boat passes through the 'eye' of the wind, the mainsail will begin filling with air on the other side. Crew weight moves as necessary to the new windward side and the main sheet is hauled in so the boat sails away on the other tack. Hauling in the jib sheet should be delayed just enough for the boat to be well past the upwind position. The jib is set as the mainsail draws to start driving the boat. If the jib is hauled in too early before the boat has turned sufficiently, the wind may hit it on the wrong side so it is 'caught aback'. Then it will push the bow back to a stationary upwind position, where it is 'in irons'.

Getting into irons is something that an expert may never admit to doing, but it can happen to any helmsman. To get out of the position, the bow has to be turned in the direction it has refused to go. One way is to use a paddle to get round. Another is to scull with the rudder — pulling the tiller across hard one way and gently returning it. The way to get round using the sails is to back the jib and use the wind to push the bow over. By this time you are probably 'making a stern board' (going backwards). It is important to remember what is happening to the rudder. As it is going backwards through the water, it needs a reverse action to what it does when going forwards, to alter the attitude of the boat the same way. It is rather like a backed jib, only in water instead of air. Once the boat has been brought round, the sails will fill and you can sail forward.

Tuning

The difference in performance between two apparently identical boats may be a matter of tuning. The leading edges of both sails are most important in windward performance. The jib loses efficiency if it sags away as a result of a slack forestay. The mainsail needs to be tight up the mast, but not strained so much that the sail creases. The correct tensioning here coupled with adjustments along the boom will ensure that the sail is set smoothly.

The pull of the main sheet and a kicking strap also contribute to sail setting. The jib is particularly sensitive to the direction of pull of its sheet. On many boats the lead of the sheet is through a fairlead which can be adjusted fore-and-aft. Experimenting with this and observing differences in the setting of the sail will show how to get the best setting and the greatest power from it.

◀ Some hulls are designed to lift partly out of the water in suitable winds and plane on part of the bottom aft. This increases speed, but careful trimming is needed to maintain the plane and avoid capsize.

Sailing in a tideway

Although sailing in non-tidal waters can be enjoyable, there is added interest in sailing where there is tidal movement. Much enjoyment and experience can be gained in large bays, harbours and inlets. An understanding of tides is necessary and this should be coupled with local knowledge. Prepare your journey thoroughly before setting out. Even in a simple inlet, you could be left on a mudbank if you did not know the tide left it. Get local advice and obtain any special publications on the waters.

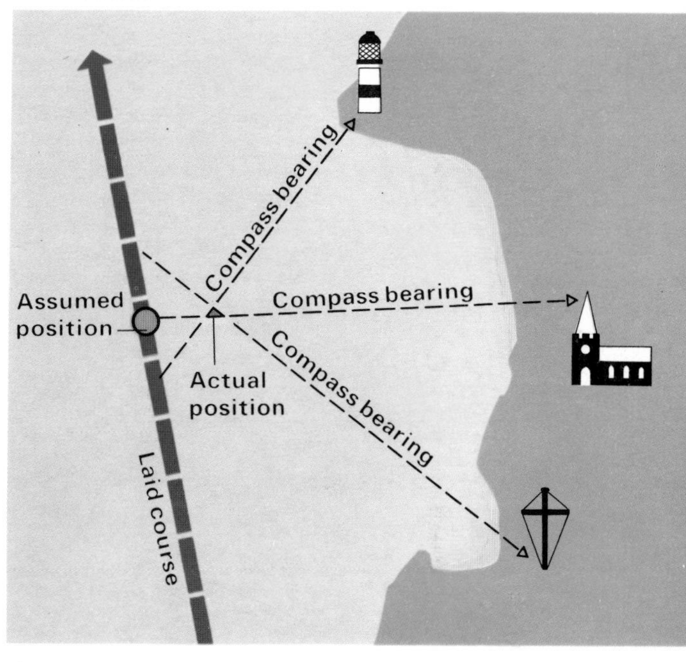

▲ Bearings of fixed objects can be transferred to the chart to get your position.

Using a chart

When sailing in a tideway, the first essential is a chart. For a large expanse of water in an area less popular for yachting, you may have to use a chart intended for larger craft. Unfortunately this may not give as much detail as desired for smaller boats. Yachtsmen's charts (if available) are best of all. They are usually in colour and have harbour plans of many places. Learn the meaning of the various symbols in the key. There may be little time for making references when afloat. Identify visible marks from the shore. Get tide times before you go afloat and note the rise and fall and what areas dry out. There are many local tide tables published additional to those in nautical almanacs. If there is a harbourmaster, seek his advice, but do not necessarily regard every man in a blue jersey as an expert.

Navigable channels for larger craft are marked in restricted waters. With your shallower craft you may be able to venture outside these. But pay particular attention to places where there is much movement of silt. There may be quite an abrupt difference in depth between a dredged channel and the bottom outside the buoys. A quickly flowing ebb tide could leave you on soft mud for six hours or more waiting for the next tide.

Sailing on moving water

When sailing in a tideway you have to take flow into account as well as the strength of the wind. Away from the shore you may not realize how quickly the water is moving. Observe its flow past fixed objects, such as buoys and moored craft, and in general sail downstream of them. Otherwise, you may be washed onto them with disastrous results, if the water is flowing fast.

Check your position and movements by observing

things ashore. You may be making good speed through the water, yet you might not be making any progress at all over the bottom if there is a strong stream the other way. This is especially so when tacking against wind and tide. You may return after a tack and find yourself no further forward in relation to a point on the shore. Your only hope may be to anchor or moor until the tide slackens. The moral is to work your tides and take them into account when planning a time of return.

▼ The deepwater channel of an inlet or tidal river is marked with buoys. They may lose their colours, so watch the shapes. Pass flat-topped can shapes on your port side and pointed conical shapes on your starboard side as you enter in the direction of the flood tide.

Chart and compass work

It is important to know where you are and where your destination is. Sea mists are possible and you may find landmarks obscured. It is not always possible to take accurate bearings in a small boat, but you should have a compass. Preferably get a small steering compass that has sights so it can double as a hand bearing one. Even a pocket compass has its uses for practise in confined tidal waters. You should be able to get directions of fixed objects with reasonable accuracy so you can relate them to your course and lines you mark on the chart.

Although your course might be only a few miles across a bay, make a practice of noting the compass bearing of your destination and check it as you progress. This knowledge could be valuable. Take bearings of landmarks ashore that are marked on the chart, and pencil these on the chart to get your approximate position where they cross. If you take three bearings it is unlikely that they will meet at a point, but you will get a little triangular 'cocked hat' in which your boat should be. You will need a roller rule or other device for transferring bearing lines from one of the compass roses on the chart.

Practise this basic pilotage in clear weather and smaller surroundings, so you know how to do it if faced with the real problem in

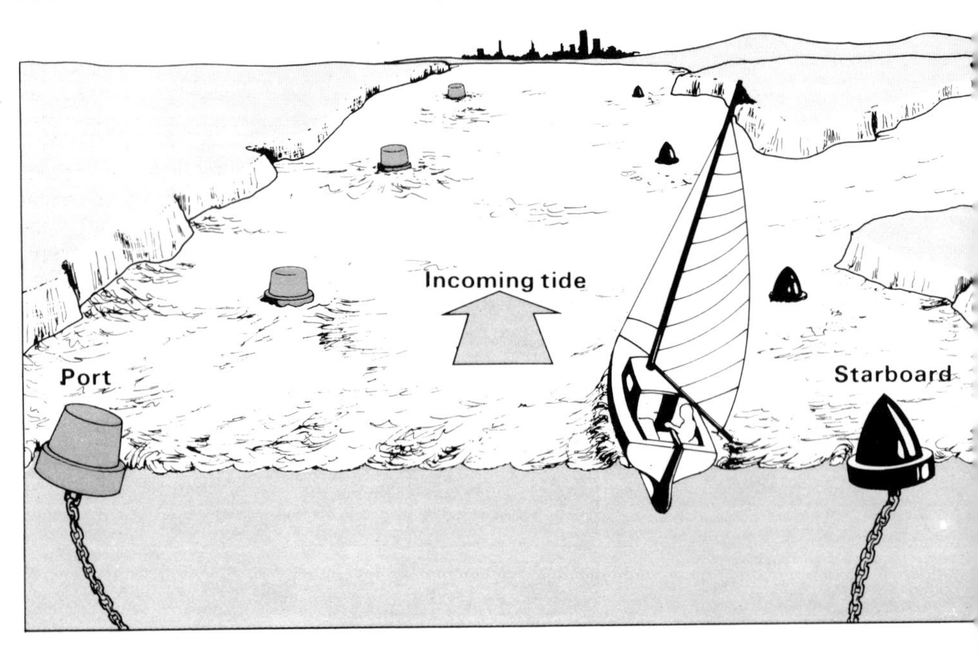

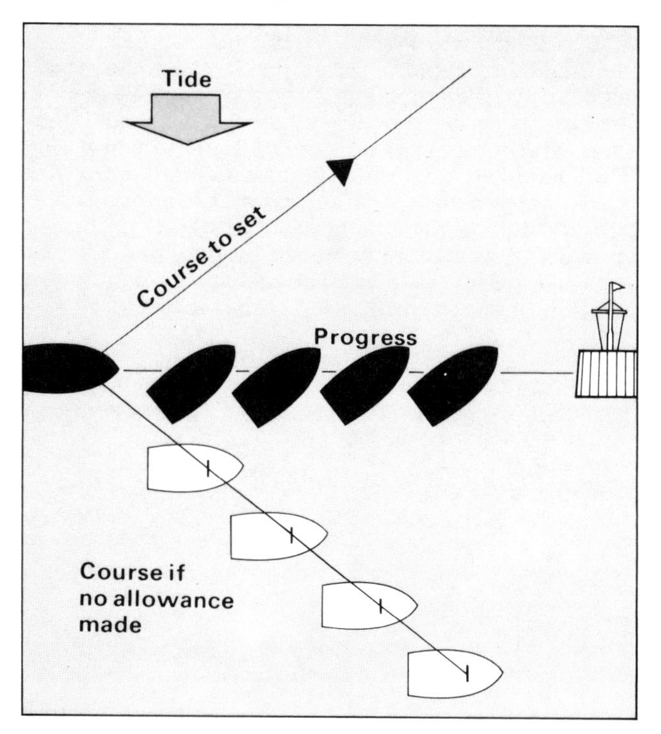

bad conditions or on a longer voyage.

▲ When sailing across a tidal stream, sufficient allowance must be made or the boat will be carried a long way off course by the tide.

Longer voyages

When sailing any distance on tidal water, you have to allow for what the movement of water will be doing to your boat. Tidal effects are negligible on a fast power boat, but the speed of a small sailing boat may not be as much as the average tide speed. The simplest examples are sailing with and against the tide. When sailing with the tide you may find you have gone as much as 40 kilometres further in six hours than if you had been sailing in still water. You would be wasting your time and getting nowhere trying to sail against such a tide. You might even lose ground although your progress through the water may seem good.

Steering a course

The effects of wind and tide have to be estimated when sailing across a tidal stream. Suppose you reckon it will take four hours to reach your destination at 5kph and there is a tidal flow averaging this speed at right-angles to your course. If you merely point the bow directly where you expect to be going, you will actually move along a course 45° to leeward of the one you set and end up 18 kilometres downstream of your destination. To correct this, you have to aim at a point 45° to windward and your progress over the bottom would actually be crabwise.

Both tidal flow and the wind are variable so you will probably have to check your position and correct your course at intervals during the voyage.

Practise all these procedures first in restricted tidal waters and this will show what is involved. More detailed pilotage and navigation knowledge will be needed when you tackle coastal cruising or go offshore.

The above example is an extreme case. There are many variations where, for instance, the intended course is diagonal to the tidal stream. The methods for dealing with these situations are outlined in the numerous books on simple navigation. Most problems can usually be solved by simple geometry on the chart. The course will have to be checked and corrected frequently as wind speed and direction may change. However, if you want to make longer journeys on tidal waters, you will need more sophisticated navigational equipment and a thorough knowledge of how to use it.

Making the boat go faster

In light airs, there is an advantage in increasing sail area. It is not often practicable to replace the mainsail with a larger one, but there can be alterations forward of the mast. A cutter can even have variations in the number of sails. Alternatively in the usual sloop rig, the jib can be changed to a larger genoa or a large light spinnaker added. In stronger winds, when a small boat is carrying more sail than can be balanced by the crew on the gunwale, it is possible to get their balancing weights further out by using trapezes.

A genoa

This is a jib with its foot about twice as long as the working jib. Besides giving extra sail area, the overlap on the mainsail has a slot effect, directing air to the reverse side of the mainsail so improving performance.

A spinnaker

There is no great advantage in using a genoa when sailing off the wind. In this position it is best to hoist a spinnaker. It is made using panels of light cloth — usually nylon—which are cut so that the sail sets in a parachute shape. Sometimes it is difficult to handle, but with a light wind abaft the beam, it makes use of all the air there is to drive the boat forward.

A spinnaker sets outside the rigging and the jib is usually lowered. The head of the sail is hoisted with a halliard and the sail boomed out with a pole to the mast. This is steadied with a guy and there is a sheet from the opposite corner. The pole is also steadied by up and down hauls from the mast. As the spinnaker is symmetrical, sides are changed by moving the pole over. When directly downwind, the spinnaker is allowed to catch all the wind it can and pull ahead. If the wind is from one side, the spinnaker is moved round like a jib.

Efficient handling of the spinnaker in racing can make a considerable difference to results. However, for cruising in anything up to a small cabin yacht, many owners would regard it as a nuisance.

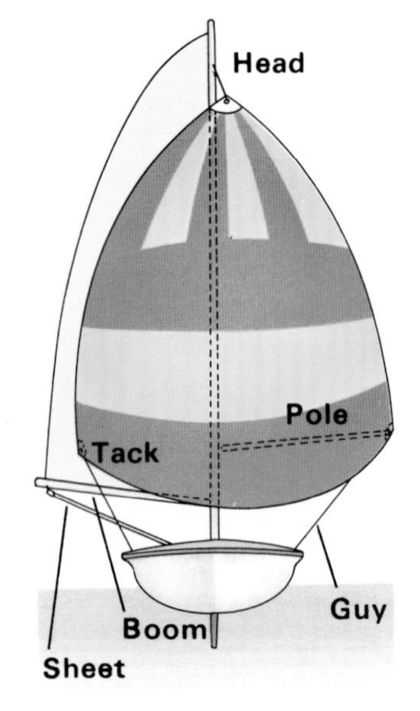

Hoisting

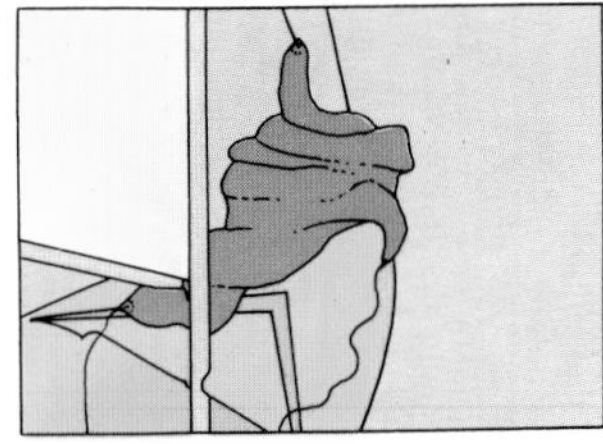

Fitting pole

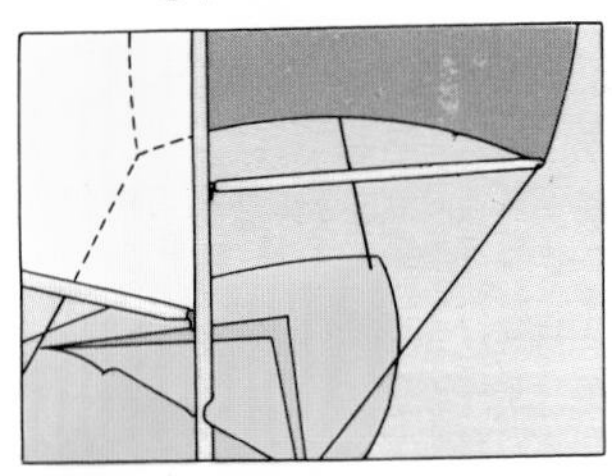

Setting

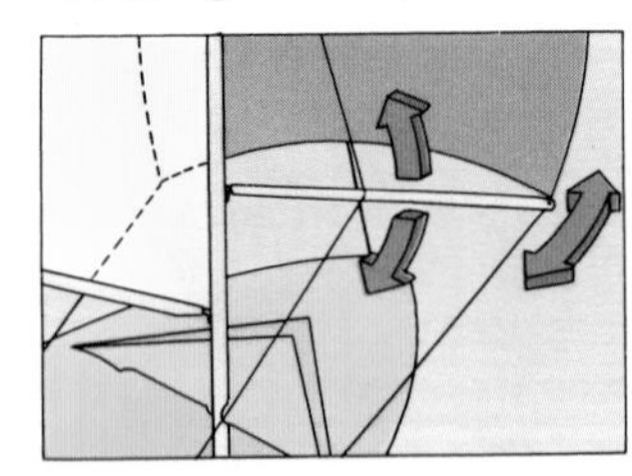

A sliding seat

In order that a small boat is able to carry more sail to make it go faster in normal or strong winds, the crew have to get their weight further out. Some racing craft have sliding seats, where a crew member can position himself right outside the gunwale with his feet on it. The seat can be slid across when going about.

A trapeze

This is a more recent method of using the crew's weight as a counter balance. It consists of a harnessed seat suspended from high on the mast. The crew sits in the seat with his feet on the gunwale. When going about, he attaches his harness to a wire on the other side. The seat and harness have a quick-release clip fixed to a handle on the wire from the mast. When the harness is released to change sides, the handle is brought to the shroud.

The crew on the trapeze still handles the jib sheet, but adjusts his weight as needed by moving in and out as he flexes his legs.

▲ A spinnaker makes use of all available wind, while the man on the trapeze uses his weight to trim the boat level.

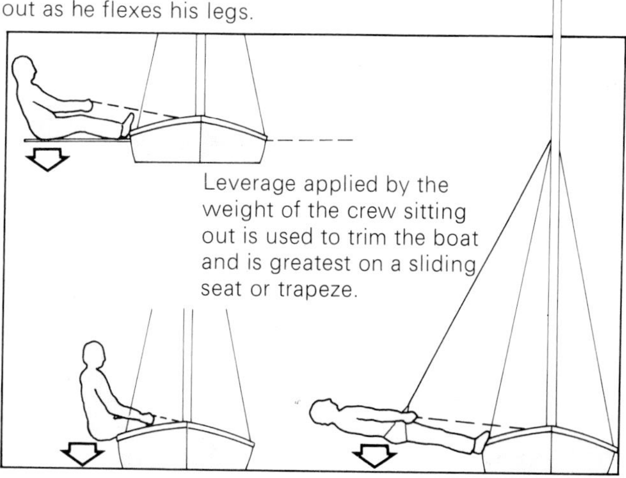

No wind

The wind does not always blow, although at sea and on large lakes there is usually some movement of air. Therefore, it is wise to have at least one other means of propulsion besides sails. Dinghies are best rowed when becalmed, but smaller craft may be paddled a short distance. Many boats can also be sculled over the stern. An outboard motor is a favoured reserve method of propulsion. It has to be kept in good order, however, and may take up valuable space when out of use. Sometimes it might even be possible to accept a tow from another boat.

Paddling and rowing

Moving a becalmed dinghy with one or two paddles is only a suitable method for a short distance, as it requires a good deal of effort. Rowing is considerably easier. Sit on a central thwart and face aft. Brace your feet against something and use your whole body to provide the pull. This is the most efficient way of converting muscle power to forward progress. And the boat may still be steered using the rudder.

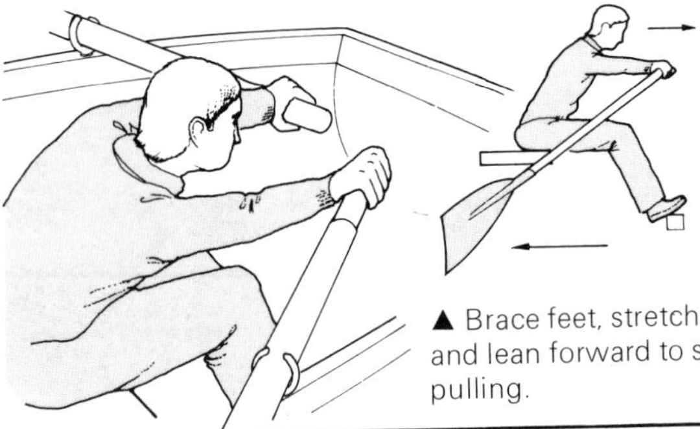

▲ Brace feet, stretch arms and lean forward to start pulling.

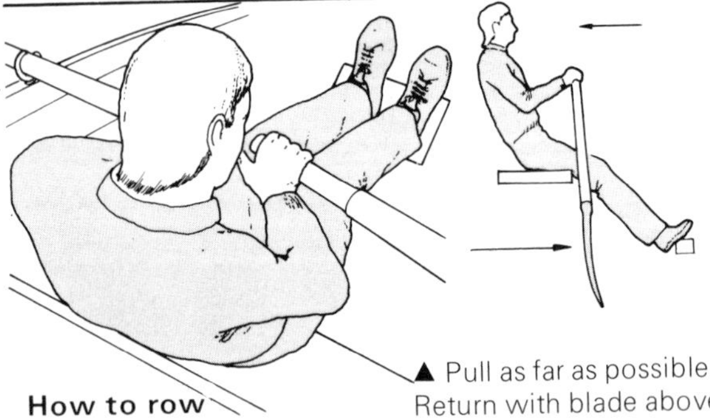

▲ Pull as far as possible. Return with blade above water.

How to row

Outboard and inboard motors

On a cabin boat, an outboard motor is best mounted on a bracket fixed to the transom and far enough to one side for the rudder still to be used. The motor can be tilted when sailing, or removed and stowed elsewhere. A small motor will lash alongside a dinghy centreboard case. The motor head should always be protected from water when not in use. An integral fuel tank makes for easier handling, but larger motors are linked by hose to separate tanks. Outboard motors are designed to suit standard transom heights of 38 or 50cm. This is measured from the underside of the mounting clamp to the underside of the hull at the motor position.

Although a loose cord may be used to start a motor, it is better to have a recoil starter. Outboards run on a mixture of petrol and oil. Exact proportions are important as running trouble is usually due to fuel or sparking plugs. Consequently, carry spare plugs and a suitable spanner.

For a cabin yacht up to about eight metres, a motor of 10HP will be adequate. Few dinghies need more than 2 HP. A small inboard motor may be considered for a cabin yacht, but it can take up valuable space.

Sculling

Most craft can be sculled over the stern providing there is a sculling notch or a mounting for a rowlock in the transom. Propelling the boat with a single oar has particular advantages in crowded moorings. The blade is drawn underwater across the stern with one face at about 45° aft. At the end of the stroke the blade is turned through 90° and drawn back through the water still keeping the same face aft. To do this, hold the end of the oar with your hand bent fully forward in one direction and fully back in the other.

Altering the angle of the blade or pulling harder one way alters the course. An oar over the stern can also make an emergency rudder and it is possible to row the stern round when quick turns are needed.

Taking a tow

There are some considerations that may not be immediately obvious if you are offered a tow by a motor boat.

The tow rope must be kept over the bow by a fairlead or a temporary lashing—a pull slipping to one side

How to scull

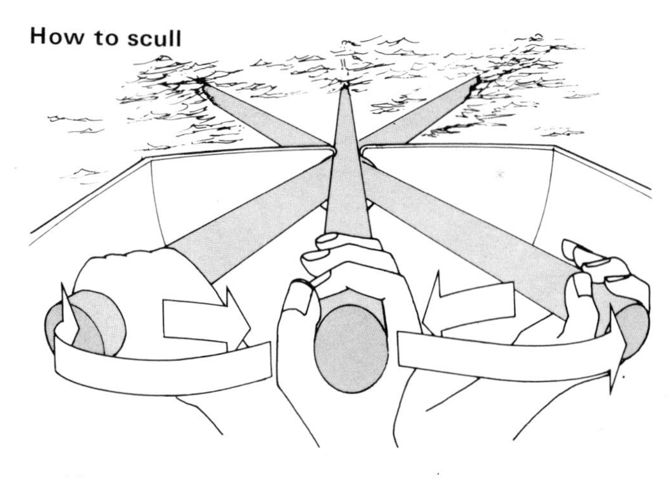

could make the boat yaw and capsize. It should be fairly long and not secured too permanently in your boat. It is better to pass a turn round the mast or a thwart and hold the end in your hand. This will enable you to let go in an emergency. If a knot is used, it should be a slippery hitch that can be cast off by pulling the rope's end.

The optimum speed of a dinghy is not as high as many motor boats, so a tow at much over the optimum speed will pull the dinghy bows under. Make sure anyone who offers you a tow realizes they must travel slowly. Be ready to slip the tow rope if they do not.

▼ There is skill in making use of the slightest breeze, but when becalmed an alternative means of propulsion is vital.

Bad weather sailing

A sailing craft is intended to suit what the designer regards as normal conditions. It is expected to have a reasonable performance with its standard rig and be safe under ordinary circumstances. Conditions are not always normal, so a sailor has to be prepared to deal with worsening weather or seas. Sail area may have to be reduced or, in severe conditions, a yacht at sea may have to heave-to. A more likely hazard for the dinghy sailor to deal with, however, is a capsize. A good seaman is one who knows how to deal with any weather condition.

Reducing sail area

Sail area has to be reduced when it becomes obvious that too much canvas is being carried for safety. Usually some sail must be retained forward of the mast, either by rolling some of the jib round the forestay, or by substituting a smaller jib. The mainsail area is reduced by gathering up some of the canvas along the foot.

Traditional reefing

In the traditional method of reefing a mainsail, there are one, two or three rows of short lanyards (reefing points) projecting each side of the sail. To take in a reef, the boat is turned head to wind and the main halliard

▼ In bad weather it is sometimes necessary to reduce the area of sail carried. This can be done by gathering up the foot of the sail or by roller reefing.

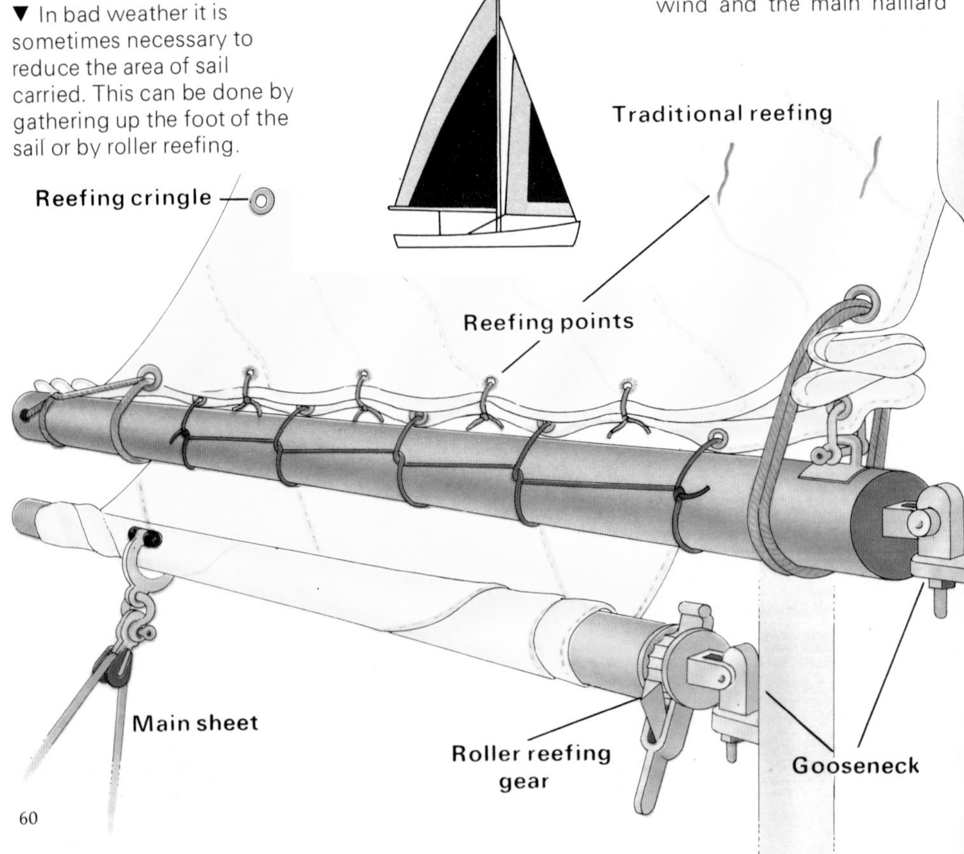

slackened. A cringle at the mast end of the line of reefing points is hauled down and secured to the tack end of the boom. At the other end of the line, a similar cringle is lashed down so the sail is stretched along the boom. This is important, or the reefing points would be subject to more strain than intended. Surplus canvas is gathered up and the reefing points tied round it with reef bows—above the boom if the sail is lashed to it or round the boom if the sail is in a groove.

Roller reefing

The traditional type of reefing has given way to roller reefing. To do this in a dinghy, slacken the main halliard and pull the boom from the square spike on the gooseneck. Turn the boom round so that the sail is rolled up to the required point and then push it back onto the gooseneck spike.

In a larger sailing yacht handling the boom in this manner would be impossible. As a result, roller reefing gear is necessary. This enables the boom to be rotated at the gooseneck using either a lever ratchet or a

▼ An efficient modern way of reefing a mainsail is to reduce sail area by rolling the foot of the sail smoothly round the boom.

worm wheel and pinion turned by a winch handle.

For the simplest operation, the sheet should be fixed to a swivel at the end of the boom. For centre sheeting or a kicking strap, there has to be a claw outside the rolled canvas. This complication is usually avoided on cruising yachts by only having end sheeting.

A Bermudan sail with roller reefing can be reduced to a very small area. A cruising yacht may carry a small, heavy canvas storm-sail to set in place of the mainsail. A gaff-headed sail can have similar boom reefing, with the gaff lowered to a new position. There is no simple method of dealing with a gunter gaff. It has to have the halliard relocated to suit the reduced sail height.

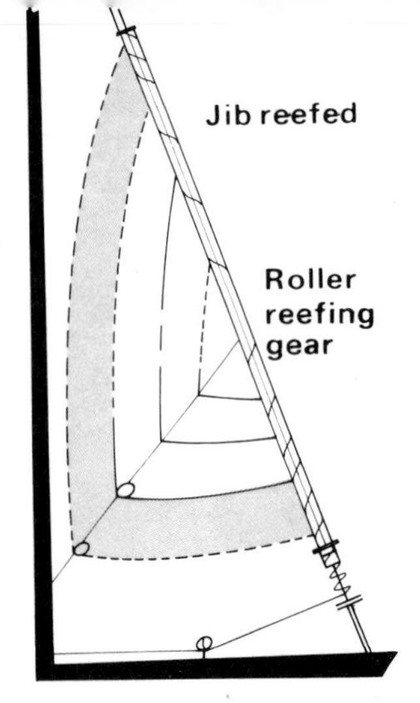

HEAVING-TO

If a cabin boat is caught in bad weather, making it unwise to sail on, the alternative is to heave-to. This is a method of stopping a boat so it is as safe as possible. It necessitates turning its head to wind and keeping it there. The boat will drift slowly downwind, however, so there must be sea room for it to do this. Heaving-to is impracticable if there is a lee shore.

A boat can be heaved-to in various ways. A small amount of mainsail on a centrally-lashed boom may do it, or a small mainsail to one side and a small jib the other side may work. The rudder is also lashed to counteract its tendency to turn off the wind. Alternatively, heavy ropes may be trailed.

These are conditions in which you should never find yourself, but it is interesting to experiment with sail settings to see how best a particular boat will heave-to.

CAPSIZING

Bad weather increases the likelihood of a dinghy capsize. Anyone who regularly sails a dinghy would be wise to practice deliberate capsizes so the recovery technique is understood and a real emergency can be dealt with calmly.

Taking precautions

In any boat where capsizing is a possibility, precautions should be taken. The sails

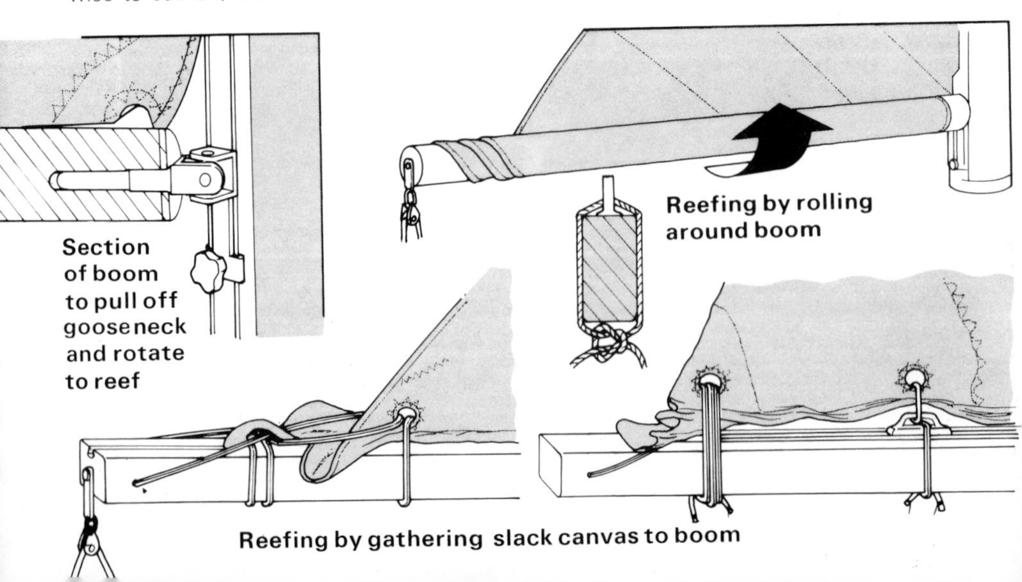

will almost certainly be set if a capsize occurs. Halliards should be made fast so they can be cast off by feel—underwater if necessary. If there are air bags, they should be secure and prevented from moving. Any loose gear should be attached to the boat or held by nets or bags. Lifejackets or buoyancy aids ought to be worn and properly secured. Should the boat go over unexpectedly, you know then that you have done all that you could to ease the situation and can get on calmly with righting the boat. In any event, stay with your boat. It is usually safer to let any gear float away rather than try to retrieve it. You may not be able to get back again.

Causes of a capsize

The causes of a capsize are many. In a sensitive boat, for example, such as a sophisticated racer, sudden overpowering, a breakage or a moment of inattention can all result in the boat going over. It may also occur because the crew make an unwise movement to leeward, or through inexperience on the part of the helmsman.

Righting the boat

If the boat has its reserve buoyancy properly disposed about the hull, it will go over so the mast and sails rest on the water and the centreboard is parallel with and a short distance above the surface. With a crew of two, one man gets onto the centreboard. To prevent breaking it his feet should be close to the hull. He leans over the gunwale and finds the jib sheet in its fairlead, then pulls the sheet through until the knot jams against it. His mate in the water steadies the boat. The man on top leans back on the jib sheet and the boat comes upright. There may be considerable suction on the sails, but they are likely to break with the water quickly. It is possible for the other man to position himself so the righting boat scoops him up. This has the advantage that he is then ready to ease anything that may be stopping the sails flapping freely. Alternatively, the man on top goes over the gunwale into the boat and the man in the water clambers in

1 A sudden unexpected gust may blow the boat over before the crew have time to ease the sheets to prevent a capsize.

2 An unexpected lull in the wind may catch the crew sitting-out too far and the boat consequently capsizes to windward.

3 It is important to get to the boat quickly after being thrown into the water. Otherwise it might be carried downwind.

4 The centreboard is used to provide righting leverage. Both crew should be ready for action as the boat comes up.

over the stern. Some of the water is bailed and the boat sailed on. An automatic bailer will remove more.

Not every capsize is straightforward but these are the basic techniques to adopt for an average sailing dinghy. The sails should be to leeward of the hull. A too buoyant hull may soon blow round the other way and any attempt to right the boat will almost certainly cause the boat to continue over and capsize again the other way. It is better for one man in the water to hold the bow to prevent the hull turning downwind, while the other man rights it.

Outside help

A boat with too little reserve buoyancy may be impossible to right normally without help. Lowering the sails may make it easier to control, but if the boat is righted to a level where the water inside is higher than the top of the centreboard case, outside help will be needed.

Sometimes a boat will turn completely over. Providing the mast is not stuck in mud, it may be possible to stand on the hull and lever on the centreboard to slowly right it. More leverage can be gained by pulling on a jib sheet from one side while leaning far out on the other.

If the mast is stuck in the mud a motor boat will have to be used to do the pulling, and so move the boat and turn it over.

Gaining experience

Capsizing is obviously something to be avoided if possible. In racing, however, it is one of the hazards regarded as a part of the thrill of the sport. Skill at sailing and a knowledge of the boat in particular are the best guards against capsizing. Avoid overcanvassing for the wind conditions and check all your gear. Make sure too that the crew know what to do or are willing to be told. The experienced man looks ahead and assesses probable conditions and how he will deal with them.

▶ One man should keep the boat positioned bow to wind, while his mate gets ready for righting on the centreboard.

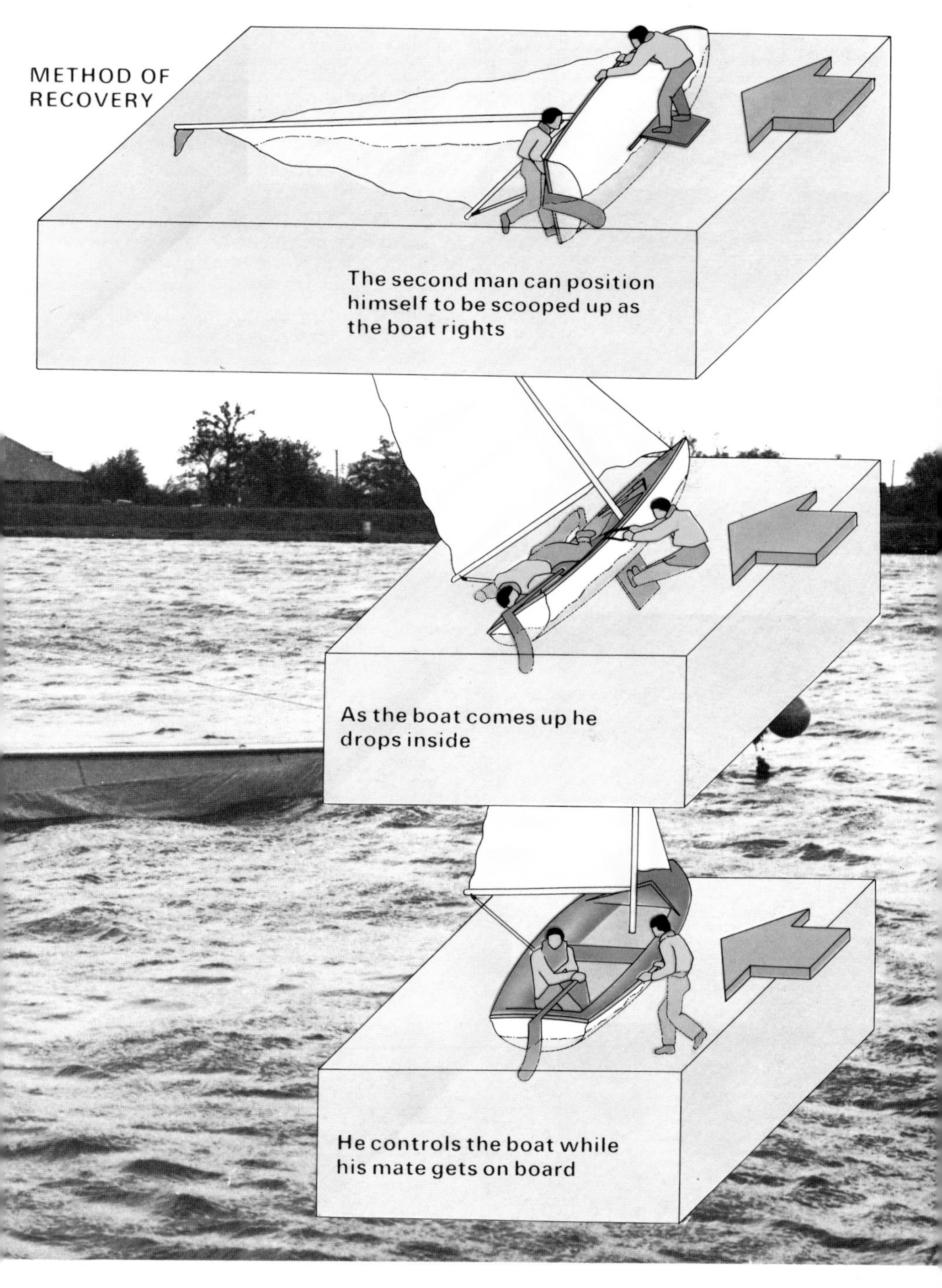
METHOD OF
RECOVERY
The second man can position
himself to be scooped up as
the boat rights
As the boat comes up he
drops inside
He controls the boat while
his mate gets on board

Rules of the road

There are internationally understood rules for preventing collisions at sea. They have been drawn up in detail to suit all circumstances, but are mostly applicable to larger craft. Anyone using a small sailing craft must apply commonsense, particularly when their intended course crosses that of a much larger vessel. The polite and sensible thing then is to keep out of the way. A large vessel cannot change course quickly and is unable to manoeuvre in a narrow channel. However, in most circumstances sailing craft have rights of way over motor boats and even rowing boats.

Oncoming craft

In general, meeting craft pass port to port and therefore keep to the right of each other. This only applies when meeting an oncoming boat—you do not have to stay on the right of a river or narrow channel. When overtaking, you can go either side, but do not interfere with the course of the other boat.

If you have the right of way, you should hold your course while the other craft takes avoiding action. Difficulty comes in racing. It would be unfair to expect traffic to stop for maybe thirty boats, each on a different course. Power craft must be allowed to get by, usually to one side and preferably astern of craft after a tack.

Dealing with collision courses

The rules governing the action a craft must take to avoid a collision must be understood for both general sailing and racing.

There are two rules to memorize for sailing craft on a collision course. When each has the wind on a different side, the vessel which has the wind on the port side must keep out of the way of the other. This means that if two boats are sailing to windward on opposite tacks, the boat with the wind on the port side must give way. It also applies if they are sailing off the wind, but with the wind on opposite sides.

When both have the wind on the same side, the vessel which is upwind (to windward) should keep out of the way of the vessel which is downwind (to leeward). For example, one boat may be close-hauled while another with the wind on the same side is running. Because the boat is upwind it must take avoiding action. This applies whatever the attitude of each vessel in relation to the wind. The exception is when they are approaching head on and both should alter course to pass port to port.

It is not always easy to know if craft on converging courses are likely to meet. When the other craft is sighted, line up parts of your rigging with it. If the other boat is still at this angle when sighted later, you are likely to collide unless avoiding action is taken. If the angle varies between sightings, the boats will cross on their courses at different times, so there is no risk.

There is no defined way

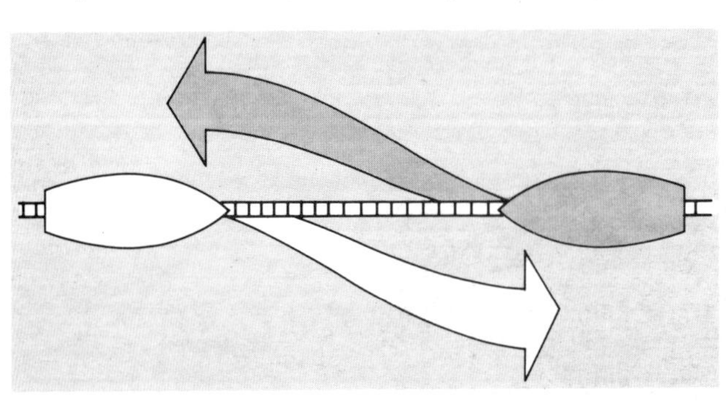

In the close quarters of racing quick thinking is necessary to interpret the rules and avoid collisions in a melée involving several boats.

for how you should avoid other craft. It will vary according to circumstances. Usually on a converging course, the boat taking avoiding action changes course to pass astern of the other. It may be necessary to bear away, gybe, or go about. Whatever you do, make it obvious to the other helmsman that you are taking avoiding action.

If you use a motor, even with the sails still set, you become a power craft. The port-to-port meeting rule applies, but if two power craft are on converging courses with a risk of collision, the one that has the other on her starboard side gives way.

◀ K116, on port tack, has to keep clear and does this by altering course to pass astern of the other boat.

Racing

Racing does not appeal to everyone who sails. It is a participation sport with a considerable following, rather than one with much spectator appeal. Enjoyment comes from pitting your skill against others, so a race is a real test of your ability. Being in a fleet of boats with their crews trying to use their knowledge of the wind, tide and current to get to the finish first is also a good way to improve your own sailing skills. It also enables you to learn some of the finer points of rules of the road.

Boats to use

It is possible to race with almost any type of sailing craft and there are often informal contests. More serious racing takes place in 'class' boats which conform to certain class rules. Racing has a long history and there are still classes of sailing that go back to the beginning of the century. However, it was the development of amateur-built, plywood boats after World War II that led to the proliferation of dinghy racing classes. Most of these classes are still in use, although glass fibre versions are used alongside the plywood ones.

Some class dinghies are designed for racing and have little use for family sailing or cruising, particularly those with a high performance. There are others, such as the Wayfarer, G.P.14 and Heron, which can put up a satisfactory racing performance, but are also used for more general sailing. Larger craft with cabins suitable for living on board may also conform to class rules and be used for racing as well as their more usual cruising.

There are two main types of racing dinghy. In a 'one-design' class, the boats and their rigs are, as near as possible, exactly alike. Only very minor variations are allowed. Boats may be all the product of one builder and they have to pass the tests of an official class

▲ Fresh water lakes, such as here at Sneek in Holland, provide reliable safe conditions for learning and racing.

▶ One of the most popular simple small craft for young people is the Optimist, which has a worldwide following.

'measurer'. Old boats in such a class do not become outdated and a race is a test of the skill of the crew only.

In a 'restricted' or 'development' class, the rules are much less limiting. They only specify points such as maximum length and sail area, with just a few other stipulations. This leaves designers considerable scope and some of the great advances in design have come through these classes. However, there is the risk that older boats in a class may not be as fast or efficient as newer ones.

Conforming to the class

When getting a boat for racing it is important to check that it conforms to its class rules. It has to be examined periodically and the measurer issues a certificate. A boat that does not conform to the rules cannot race, although it may still be used for general sailing. If you are interested in a restricted class, an old boat may not give a very creditable performance, though it may be useful for learning. Check what boats are acceptable at the club where you hope to race.

Boats of more than one class may race against each other. So that handicapping

can be arranged fairly, there is a system of 'yardstick numbers' for most established classes. A list of these numbers is issued by the Royal Yachting Association and they indicate relative capabilities, from the 140s for general-purpose boats down to the 80s for extreme racers.

Number of crew

The number of people aboard for dinghy racing is specified. There are single-handed classes, but most racing dinghies carry two. The helmsman usually refers to his companion as 'crew'. Only a few of the larger dinghies carry more than two. With cabin craft that are used for class racing, the number of crew is rarely specified.

The course

Courses for racing are laid out round buoys or other marks. The shape of the course may depend on the available water, particularly on some of the smaller lakes used for dinghy racing. Natural features may also dictate the course. For lengthy races on open water the course may be round an island or navigation marks.

A triangular course is normally adopted wherever possible. This is arranged so the first leg is to windward, therefore encouraging the boats to spread out, so relieving congestion round the first buoy. It also makes it easier to keep boats in place behind the starting line. The three legs of a triangular course also provide a test of skill in sailing upwind, reaching and running.

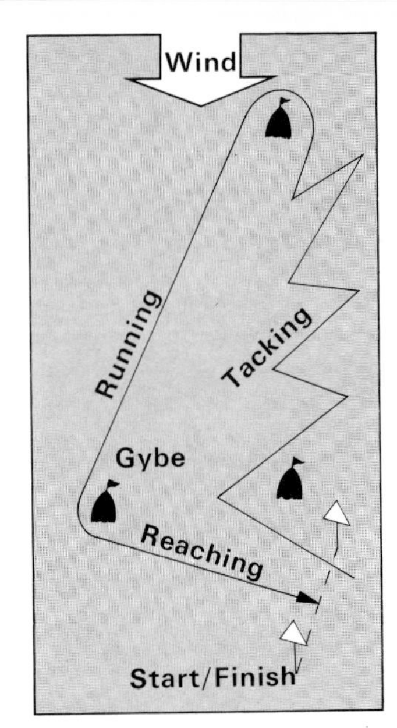

▲ Racing courses vary. Many have three stages which test the crew's skill at tacking, running and reaching.

The race

The start is across a line between marked points, with the course to windward of it. There should be enough space behind for the boats to manoeuvre. The starter and other officials are stationed at one end of the line, and are equipped with flag signals and a starting gun. Each class is allocated a flag in the International Code—a series of alphabetical and other flags used primarily for signalling between ships at sea.

Boats go afloat sometime before the start of the race. Ten minutes before starting there is a sound signal, usually a gun, then the class flag is broken out. This is followed by a five-minute gun and the International Code flag 'P' which puts all the competitors under 'starter's orders'. During this time the boats jockey for position while carefully watching the time left before the start. At the start there is a final sound signal and both the class and 'P' flags are hauled down.

Other signals can be used to recall one or several boats which may cross the line too early. If the wind changes in strength or dies completely, further signals are used to indicate course changes or even cancellation.

A gun is fired when the winner crosses the line. Careful timekeeping is important in a handicap event, because the overall winner may not be the one home first.

The finer points

Racing is much more than just sailing a boat fast. It involves reading the wind and water conditions so advantage can be taken of eddies or wind off banks and trees. The skill and experience you build up will then help decide whether it is best to take several short tacks or perhaps fewer long ones.

Good teamwork aboard between the two crew may gain important seconds. Particularly in rounding marks, sails may have to be changed or a spinnaker set. Close teamwork ensures the boat is properly trimmed and the sails and sheets are adjusted precisely. Anticipation of changing conditions and swift response to them are the keys to a race-winning combination.

Racing rules

Successful racing requires an understanding of the rules. These are basically the rules of the road that apply to craft in close proximity anywhere, with a few variations to suit racing conditions. Helmsmen manoeuvre their boats according to the rules—collisions must be avoided. If you put another boat into a position where it has to give way, you will gain an advantage. Successful jockeying for the right of way round marks can make quite a difference to the final positions of the boats.

In the excitement of a race not everyone interprets the rules correctly. If a helmsman thinks he has not finished as well as he should because of someone else's fault, he can make a protest to the race committee. The final result of a race may not be known until corrected times have been calculated in a handicap event and any protests have been considered and settled.

▶ There are racing classes to suit all degrees of skill. The Daring is an example of a sporty racing keel-boat.

Cruising

Much enjoyment can be had by sailing to a specific destination. The trip might last just a few hours, a whole day or involve one or more overnight stops. The water may be a large harbour or loch, or a coastal passage between ports. Alternatively it could be a lake or river, or a system of inland waterways. The experienced boatman may even aim for a foreign destination.

Size of boat

The size of the boat affects cruising possibilities. For open sea use, the boat should be more than 4·5m long. If it has a cabin with enough space to live on board, it is unlikely to be less than five metres. But a longer boat would be even better.

Anything shorter than 4·5m may be suitable for sheltered tidal waters, but the smallest sailing dinghies are only suitable for placid inland waters.

For ,normal cruising, the boat should be stable and comfortable, rather than fast, although it should have a reasonable performance. Attempting to cruise with a racing boat of too high a potential may be exhilarating for short periods, but the need to sit out and the risk of capsize make it unsuitable for lengthy passages.

◀ Available sailing water varies in type between countries. British lakes are mostly small, and few rivers allow sailing very far. But coastal cruising is good. Many of the European countries have larger and more extensive rivers, while the Netherlands and Finland have extensive lakes, many of which are joined by rivers and canals. Large waters favour cabin craft as fixed keels need deep water. More restricted waters suit dinghies since centreboard craft can go almost anywhere.

Overnight stops

The internal layout of a dinghy has to be considered if you are going to sleep on board. In order to get adequate accommodation the boat should be more than 3·5m long. You can improvise in something smaller but a very small dinghy is rather spartan and uncomfortable, particularly in bad weather. Obviously if you plan to camp ashore this gets round these problems.

Mooring

A small boat does not give a very restful night on the open sea, so it is best to spend it in shelter. You might be able to haul a small dinghy onto a beach, while a cabin boat is best anchored in a sheltered place such as a harbour or creek. Remember to consider tidal movements and how you will get away next morning. Inland it is best to moor under the lee of a bank, or head-to-wind alongside the bank.

Sleeping

A small cabin yacht will almost certainly have reasonably comfortable sleeping arrangements. There should also be provision for cooking, a toilet and enough storage space if the cruise is going to last several days.

Similar arrangements in a dinghy will have to be improvised. Air beds make good mattresses for sleeping on. Put them on boards laid along the thwarts. This will keep them clear of the small amount of bilge water that inevitably rests on the bottom of the boat.

A tent can be arranged over the boom. Its aft end may be supported by the topping lift, but a central pole at the transom or shear legs from the side decks or corners of the transom give a more rigid support. The forward end of the boom may be at the usual gooseneck position. Additional headroom can be obtained by raising it to a slightly higher fitting on the mast. The aft end is best higher than the forward end, so the stern will swing downwind if the boat is anchored or at a buoy. The tent should be taken down to cleats or hooks outside the gunwales (or the coamings if there are side decks) so any water runs outside. The forward end of the tent is best carried to the bow even when there is a foredeck, while the aft end may be left open. But there should be doors to lace shut in bad weather or when the boat has to be left unattended.

Equipment

Trim has to be considered when positioning equipment in the boat. Really heavy items are best kept near the middle when sailing, and weight under a foredeck should be balanced by something aft.

Keep the boat's gear in good condition. On an extensive cruise carry suitable spare rope for replacing halliards or sheets and some sailcloth, with thread, needles and palm for sail

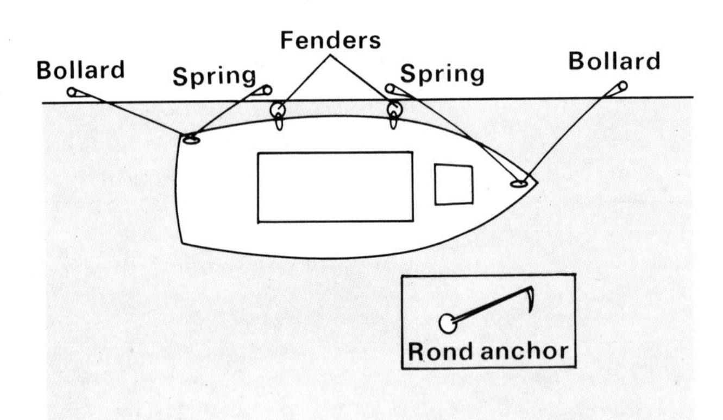

Mooring
When a boat is to lay alongside a bank, the main mooring ropes are best carried out at acute angles. If the bow is head to the stream, a spring makes the boat lay more comfortably. Where there are no suitable mooring points, rond anchors can be driven into the bank.

repairs. Stouter canvas and suitable adhesive are useful for hull repairs, although self-adhesive plastic strip can be put over a crack or used to bind broken woodwork. Have a clasp knife with a marline spike and a few tools such as pliers, screwdriver and hammer, together with the means of changing plugs and making adjustments to an outboard motor, if you take one.

Water inside a boat is a nuisance, particularly when you prepare to sleep on board. Carry a bilge pump, or at least a bucket and scoop-type bailer. A sponge may finish the job if you have to put an air bed right in the bottom.

Keeping equipment dry
In a fully open dinghy, it is difficult to keep kit dry. Handling wet bags is a nuisance when preparing for the night. Lockers under a foredeck or decks provide additional protection for waterproof bags. Nets or canvas flaps can be used to keep things in place.

Safety precautions
Everybody on board ought

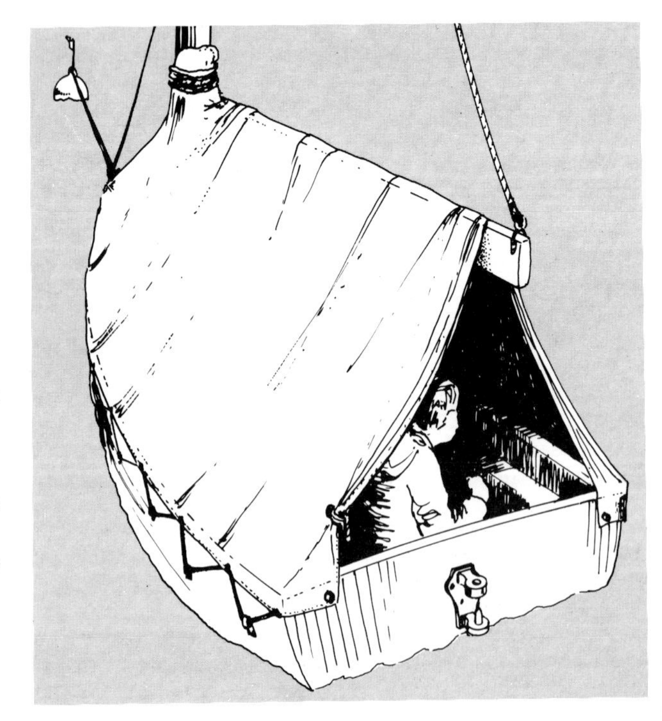

▶ With a tent slung over the boom and laced outside the gunwales, a dinghy will swing head to wind and provide a snug mooring for the night.

to have a lifejacket or buoyancy aid and, on a decked boat, wear a safety harness when going forward. In emergencies, there should be a lifebuoy to throw to the person in the water and a first aid kit to deal with burns and cuts. Also take with you a fire extinguisher suitable for tackling cooker or motor fires.

Distress flares should be carried when coastal cruising. You may have a gas lantern for use at night, but a good torch is essential as well for signalling help. On open water you need to make a noise when in fog. The easiest method is to blow on a horn or get the type connected to an aerosol.

Even if you have an outboard motor, include oars if you are going some way from shore. On inland waters, paddles may be all you need. Have a boathook for pushing off the bottom or a bank. It could be a telescopic type or a more substantial wooden pole.

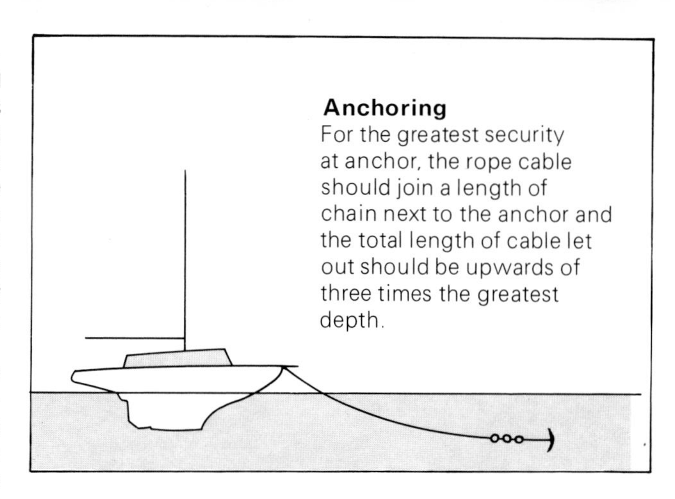

Anchoring
For the greatest security at anchor, the rope cable should join a length of chain next to the anchor and the total length of cable let out should be upwards of three times the greatest depth.

Preparations

Preparation is an important part of cruising. Get together all the guide books, maps, charts, tide tables and other information concerning the area that interests you and study them prior to setting out. If you intend cruising offshore, or in a large bay, decide on the places you wish to visit and work out courses on them beforehand. Visualize landmarks and go over the projected journey in your mind.

For open water, you must have a compass, but even on inland waters it is helpful, particularly in locating your position on a meandering river.

Have a good stock of food and water. There should be a reserve enough for a few meals although you expect to be alongside a bank every night. Water is heavy and is best carried in several plastic containers, which can be positioned where they best act as ballast. A single large container is not as easy to stow so it does not affect trim. Cabin craft normally have bottled-gas cookers. A small gas camping stove is suitable for a dinghy. Make sure petrol for an outboard motor is well out of the way for safety.

Planning the journey

When cruising, it is almost impossible to keep to a rigid timetable—you have an unknown factor in the wind. The enjoyment is lost if you have to drop sails and resort to oars or a motor to get to a place planned in advance.

When cruising round the coast you will be watched by the coastguards. Inform them when you leave and say where you hope to go. You must also tell them when you arrive or if you change your plans, otherwise an unnecessary search may be started. On inland waters, these precautions may be unnecessary, but it is wise to report your progress by telephone to someone at home every few days.

Dealing with locks

On some large rivers there is the problem of dealing with locks which might occur every few kilometres. Usually they are worked by a keeper, but on some waterways you have to work them yourself.

A lock is a water lift which enables a boat to be raised or lowered from one level to another. When you arrive at one, lower your sails. If the water inside is at your level, open the gates and move the boat in, then close the sluices. Open the ones at the other end to allow the water to rise or fall to the level outside. Open the other gates and take your boat out. Where the water level in the lock is wrong when you arrive, moor and alter the level to the same as your arrival side. Then take the boat in and carry on as before.

Never have sluices open at both ends of the lock at the same time. This merely allows water to run right through, which may not matter on a full river, but could be wasteful on a canal. In order to conserve water and lessen the work involved in operating the lock, it is best that boats go through in alternate directions. Therefore if you meet another boat coming from a lock, you should get there to find it in your favour, ready to enter.

▶ When passing through a lock, particularly with other craft, adequate fendering is needed as the boat rises or falls.

Locks
Most locks have double gates with 'paddles' to allow water to pass through when they are raised. There may be more 'paddles' set in the banks. When the gates are shut at both ends, the 'paddles' are used to adjust the water level so a boat may be raised or lowered from one water level to the other. Gates are pushed open with the 'balance beam' when the water level is the same both sides of them.

SEAFIELD

Buoyage

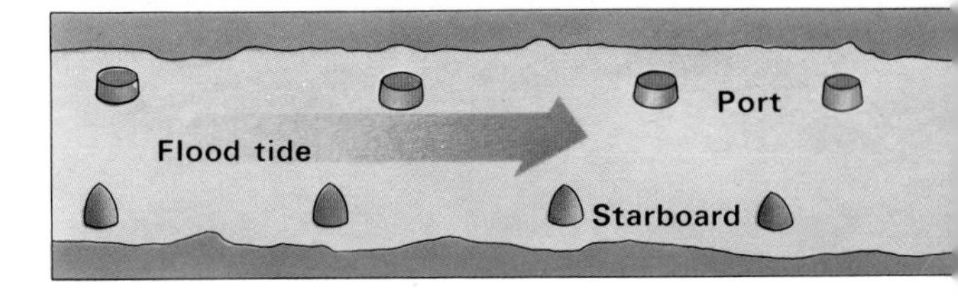

Navigation buoys

Buoys anchored to the bottom of a channel are used as navigational aids. For example, in a river estuary the navigable section is marked with red can-shaped buoys on the port side, as you enter with a flood tide, and black conical buoys on the other. Wrecks are at present marked with green conical buoys. Shape is more easy to recognize than colour. There may be a top mark in the form of a small can over a port-hand buoy or a cone over a starboard-hand one. Some buoys are marked at night with red or green flashing lights. A chart will show the positions of buoys and the rhythm of the lights.

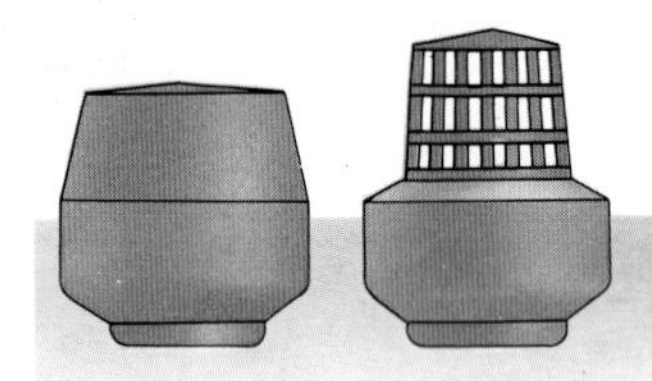

Starboard-hand buoys

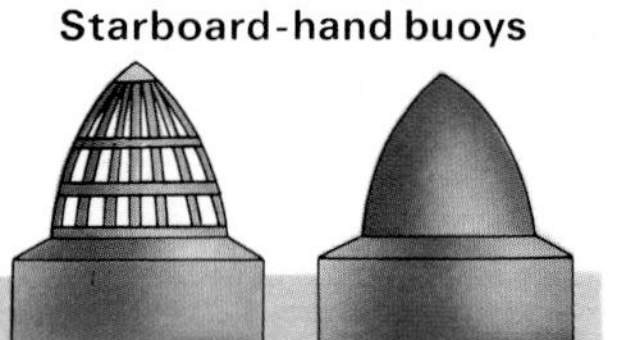

In smaller channels, posts may be used instead of buoys. These should have similar top marks to the buoys and be coloured according to the side of the channel, but some 'perches' are merely rough tree branches pushed into the mud.

Cardinal marks

Isolated dangers, and sometimes bends in a channel, may be marked with buoys of the cardinal system, painted yellow and black. Direction from the point of danger is indicated by the arrangements of pairs of conical top marks. If the two point upwards, the buoy is to the north of the hazard, if they point downwards, it is to the south. West is indicated by the cones pointing towards each other, and east has their bases together.

Other buoys

Buoys of different patterns and colours are used for other purposes and details of these will be found on charts and in pilot books. The most important buoys for the small boat sailor are those that mark channels.

It is an offence to moor to a navigation buoy. Buoys intended for mooring are different shapes and have rings where ropes can be attached, or are otherwise obvious.

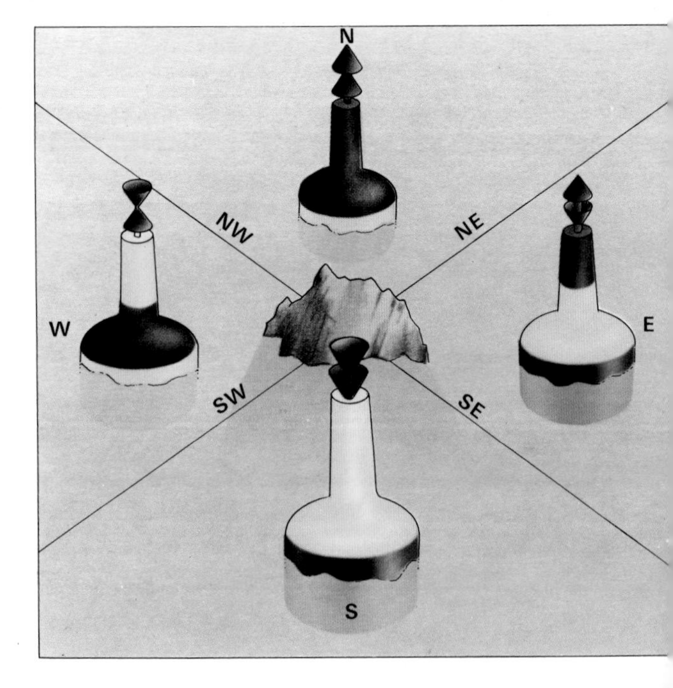

Lights

Sailing craft

When sailing after dark, it is important that you understand the lights on other craft, as well as show the correct ones yourself. The arrangement of lights indicate the type of craft and the direction in which it is moving.

In the smallest craft, you are required to show a white light in an emergency. A torch shining on a sail helps to make you seen.

Other craft under sail only have red port and green starboard lights, screened to show through the required angles. A single combined lantern is acceptable in the bow of small sailing craft. As low side lights may be difficult to see, optional tri-colour lights may be shown on the masthead.

Power craft

If an engine is used with sails, the same lights should be shown as for a full-powered craft. Besides the red and green side lights on power craft, there are white mast and stern lights, visible through the angles shown. If the vessel is over 46m, there is a second higher mast light. Additional lights indicate towing, fishing and other operations.

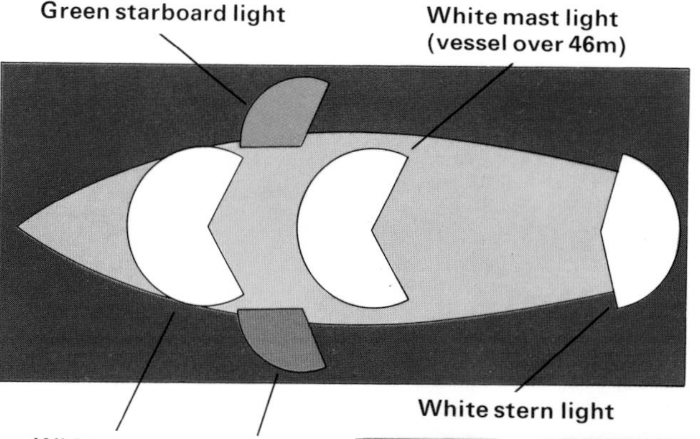

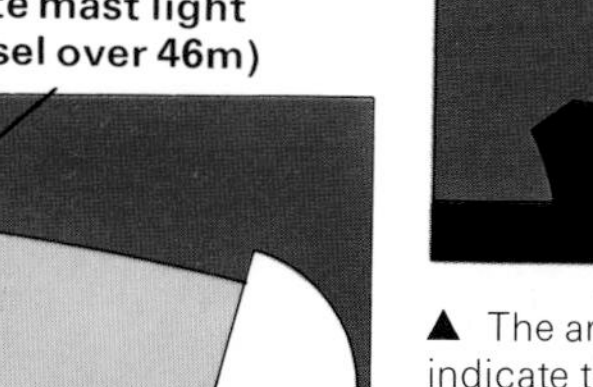

▲ The arrangements of lights indicate that a power vessel over 46m long is approaching at an angle with the port side towards the viewer.

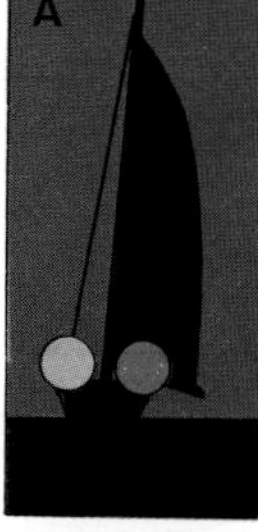

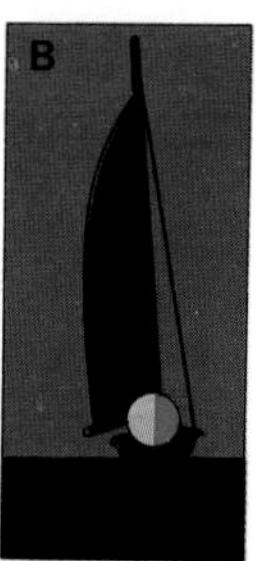

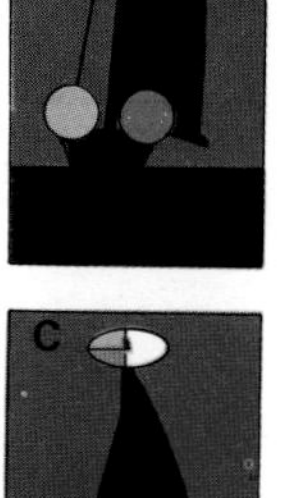

► Green and red lights without white lights indicate a sailing vessel approaching bow-on (A). Green and red lights close together indicate a combined lantern in a bow of a small yacht approaching bow-on (B). A red light, with no other lights visible indicates a yacht crossing to the left of the viewer. A green light indicates a yacht crossing to the right of the viewer. As side lights may be hidden by waves, sailing craft may, alternatively, have a combined (tri-colour) lantern at the masthead, showing a white stern light as well as side lights (C and D).

▲ There do not have to be any fixed lights in a dinghy, but a white light visible all round should be shown in an emergency.

▲ An anchored vessel less than 46m long shows a white all round light forward, hung in the rigging. A larger vessel has another lower light aft.

Tides and currents

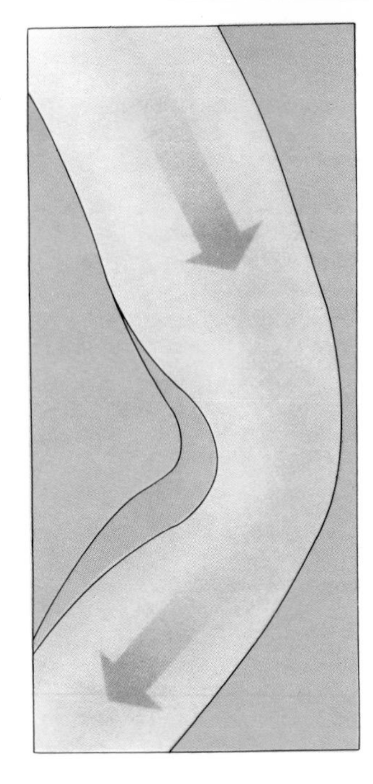

▲ The fastest flow in a river gouges out the deepest channel. On a bend the current sweeps to the outside of the curve and there may be a shallow build-up of mud and silt downriver of the inside of the bend.

Tides

In most parts of the world the sea flows round the coast one way for about six hours, then in the reverse direction for another six. This causes the rise and fall observed at any seaside place. The rising tide is the 'flood', the receding tide the 'ebb'. At about the times of full and new moon the water rises higher and drops lower to form a 'spring tide'. Midway between, the water does not rise as high or drop as low and this is a 'neap tide'.

The time interval between high tides is about 12 hours and 20 minutes, so tide times are repeated at about fortnightly intervals. In most places, the ebb tide takes a little longer than the flood tide. In both directions, the fastest flow is at half tide. 'Slack water', when there is no movement, occurs at high and low tide. A convenient proportion to remember for the relative speeds of the tide at each hour is 1:2:3: 3:2:1.

Round the British Isles the main flood tide comes from the south west. At Land's End it divides to go up the English Channel and the Irish Sea. The further a coastal place is from the dividing point, the later is its time of high water. Tide times are based on certain key places called standard ports, the most important of which is Dover. Other places have constants to be added to or subtracted from the time of high water there.

The amount of rise and fall varies considerably round the coast, from a few metres along much of the south coast to 15 metres in the Bristol Channel. Local tide tables and predictions in nautical almanacs give times, heights and other information about tides for every day.

Using a tide can add appreciably to the distance covered. Trying to sail against it may result in going backwards in relation to the ground, although still progressing forward through the water.

Of course, tidal streams are not all straight lines. They are affected by shallows and coastal outlines, and charts indicate lines of flow. One of the most notable deflections of streams round the British coast is due to the Isle of Wight. This breaks the flood tide to produce a double high water, felt as far west as Poole Harbour. Local knowledge, or careful study of the tidal stream marked on a chart, may indicate how lesser eddies can be used to get the benefit of reverse flows.

River currents

In non-tidal rivers with any noticeable flow, the fastest current is at the centre or over the deepest channel. Friction against a shallow bottom or a bank slows the flow. At a bend, the main flow sweeps outward and scours the outside. There is often a very shallow part, due to the build-up of silt at and below the inside of the curve.

When river sailing, the deep channel gives the greatest help if your course is downstream. But when sailing upstream, there may be less flow to contend with if the deepest part is avoided. However, it is unwise to go too far into the shallows as some water is drawn along by the hull and this drags on the bottom to produce a slowing effect.

When sailing upstream in a relatively narrow river with the wind ahead, better progress may result from reaching across instead of trying to point as close to the wind as possible. This builds up your best speed. Go about slowly to gain the maximum amount of progress as you shoot up into the wind. And delay falling off to the other tack until there is only just enough way left on the boat.

Weather forecasts

It is wrong to think that the only part of the weather that should concern you is the wind. Other things, such as sun and temperature, and rain and cloud, are all interrelated. Consequently you can interpret much from a forecast if the general picture is understood. Coastal and shipping forecasts are of more use than those intended for the general public. No part of Britain is far from the sea, in weather terms. For instance, a dinghy sailor on a reservoir in the Midlands can discover what weather to expect from a Bristol Channel weather forecast if the wind is in the prevailing south-westerly direction.

Personal observations

To some extent you can make a forecast from your own observations, but without the help of reports from elsewhere you are unlikely to get more than approximate accuracy for a few hours ahead. A barometer is the most useful instrument for individual forecasts. It is not a single reading, but the speed at which it rises or falls that indicates changes in weather. So a series of readings have to be taken and noted. If there is little change in barometric pressure, the weather is unlikely to change. A quick rise may mean rain, but it also means a rising wind.

The sky is probably more use for personal forecasts than a barometer. Some of the old sailor's rhymes have a foundation of fact—a red sky at night usually does mean calm weather next day. Cloud movement, or lack of it, will indicate weather and wind. Most people know what thunder clouds look like, as well as black rain clouds. The movement and type of other clouds may also indicate weather changes, but a specialist book on the subject should be consulted.

Professional forecasts

It is the job of meteorologists to collect and interpret information about the weather. As their forecasts are based on widely collected data, they are more reliable than your own. You can telephone a large number of meteorological offices (see telephone directory) and RAF stations in order to get the current forecast. The BBC regularly broadcast weather reports for shipping on 1500m. On most days they are at 00.03, 06.30, 13.55 (11.55 Sundays) and 17.55, but these times should be checked in the *Radio Times*. Gale warnings are broadcast as they are issued. Local radio stations also give reports but broadcast on the medium wave. Those based on the coast usually give reports for the sea area covered by the station. Some will even supply forecasts and observations of present conditions by telephone. (Again, consult a telephone directory or a nautical almanac for the number.) Broadcasts concerning Irish waters are made by Radio Eireann Times for these bulletins together with those of the BBC and adjacent foreign stations are also given in a nautical almanac.

Shipping areas

Forecasts for shipping round the British Isles are related to a standard chart of the surrounding sea areas. An appreciation of the weather in these areas and how it can be expected to move gives a clue to the weather that is approaching any part of Britain. Blank charts can be obtained for plotting particular forecasts as they are received.

The weather forecaster's language

Certain words used in forecasts have more precise meanings than they have in normal usage. For instance, 'imminent' is within 6 hours, 'soon' is 6 to 12 hours. A number of abbreviations are used possibly giving the impression that there is a special meteorological language. This is not really the case but rather an attempt to put a lot of information into concise form so it can be passed quickly. Detailed information on weather forecasts, their availability through radio and telephone, and how to make the best use of the information can be found in **Reed's Nautical Almanac** and in booklet G5 **Weather Forecasts** issued by the Royal Yachting Association, free to members or at a fee to non-members.

Visual warnings

Before the advent of rapid communications, visual gale warnings were displayed at ports round the British coast. These may still be seen and should be understood. The signal consists of a large cone. Warning of a gale expected from north of an east-west line is given when it is hoisted with its point upwards. If it is hoisted with its point downwards, the gale is expected from south of the line. At night there may be three lights, usually all red, arranged in a triangle in the same direction as the cone would be in daylight.

Knots are nautical miles per hour. A nautical mile is longer than a statute mile and 20 nautical miles are about 23 statute miles (about 37km).

Acquiring a boat

The best way to discover what new and secondhand boats are available is to study the advertisement pages of yachting magazines. Craft may also be seen and compared at boat shows. The major ones are held at Earls Court, London, in January; at Southampton, in early autumn; and at the Dinghy Exhibition, London, in March. If dinghy racing appeals to you, check on the classes sailed at your club before buying a boat.

Nearly all new, professionally-built craft are constructed completely of glass fibre, or with wood trim. Check what is being offered and that you do not have to pay extra for sails or other essential equipment.

BUILDING YOUR OWN BOAT

If you want to build your own boat, you have the choice of several materials and methods. Information from the sources listed will show what is available.

Boats from wood

Building a wooden boat by the traditional clinker or carvel methods is beyond the skill of most amateur craftsmen, but a satisfactory craft can be constructed from marine grade plywood.

When building in plywood, it is possible to start from scratch, or use a kit. The kit may be just a collection of wooden sections. Alternatively, some parts, such as frames, transom and stem, may be already made or all the shaping done and screw holes drilled. If someone else does this work for you, it has to be paid for. A kit supplier may save something with bulk buying, but the cheapest way to build is from materials bought locally. If you want quicker results, or do not trust your own

THE BEAUFORT SCALE				
Beaufort number	Wind speed Knots	Kmph	Description	Sail carried
0	-1	-1	Calm	Full sail, just steerage
1	1-3	1-5	Light air	Full sail
2	4-6	6-11	Light breeze	Full sail
3	7-10	12-19	Gentle breeze	Full sail
4	11-16	20-28	Moderate breeze	Smaller jib
5	17-21	29-38	Fresh breeze	1st reef in mainsail
6	22-27	39-49	Strong breeze	2nd reef, storm jib
7	28-33	50-61	Moderate gale	Well reefed
8	34-40	62-74	Fresh gale	Storm jib, trisail or sea anchor

workmanship, a kit might well be your choice. However, it may not be as satisfying to put together as building everything yourself. Another advantage of building from scratch is being able to buy materials as you need them and so spread the cost. Most kits have to be bought as one lot.

Some boats up to about four metres may be 'stitch and glue' with glass fibre tape covering the wired plywood edges. Some plans are available showing the plywood shapes, or kits may be bought with the plywood panels already shaped. Other dinghies and most larger plywood craft are built upside down on frames. These are usually fixed to the workshop floor until the hull is completed, so there must be sufficient space to allow you to work on it easily. When the hull is finished, it is usually possible to move the boat and store it away between working sessions.

Boats from glass fibre

There are now more glass fibre boats than any other type in use. But glass fibre is used mostly in professional boatbuilding as it is more suited to quantity production than the building of single boats. It is possible, however, to hire a mould for some dinghies. Although there are methods of building in glass fibre without the construction of a plug and mould in the accepted way, these methods are more suitable for larger craft. Consequently it is advisable to buy a hull and complete the fitting out and preparations for sailing yourself. This involves a considerable amount of work and although you cannot claim to have built the boat yourself you can save a lot of money.

Costs and the time factor

The amount of work and the cost of a boat is proportional to its size, which is not just a matter of length—a longer boat is also wider and deeper, with larger sections.

If you build your own sailing dinghy, including the wooden spars, but with professionally-made sails, about one-third of the work is in making the hull, and one-third in fitting this out, including rudder and centre-board. The other third is in rigging. Cost is roughly in the same proportion, except bought metal spars will save on time but add considerably to your outlay. Making sails will add to labour, but reduce their cost appreciably.

With a cabin boat, fitting out requires more time depending on how finished the interior is intended to be.

The amount of work in building a boat depends more on forward planning than is often realized. If you have all you need and you know what to do, the maximum can be gained from a given working period. The overall time can be reduced by working in a few long periods rather than a great many short ones.

PLANS

Boat Plans Ltd,
Poole,
Dorset BH17 7BH

Clyne,
250 Runnymede Avenue,
Bournemouth,
Dorset BH11 9SR.

Ditchfield Designs,
268 Priory Road,
Southampton SO2 1LS.

W. F. Harrison,
7 Scott Street,
Keighley,
West Yorkshire BD21 2JJ.

Hartley's Boat Plans,
The Croft, Polvarth Road,
St Mawes,
Cornwall.

Bruce Roberts (UK) Ltd,
73 High Street,
Bexley,
Kent.

BOAT KITS

Bell Woodworking Co. Ltd,
Narborough Road South,
Braunstone,
Leicestershire.

Cruiser Kits,
Bungay,
Suffolk.

Express Boating Organisation,
Howard Chase,
Basildon,
Essex SS14 3BD.

Jack Holt Ltd,
The Embankment,
Putney,
London SW15 1LB.

Mirror Boats,
79 Camden Road,
London SW1 9WT.

Tratman and Lowther Ltd,
Berkeley Place,
Clifton,
Bristol.

Wyvern Boats (Wessex) Ltd,
Park Street,
Yeovil,
Somerset.

York Marinecraft,
Worthington Street,
Bradford,
West Yorkshire BD8 8HB.

GLASS FIBRE HULLS

Colvic Craft,
Wheaton Road,
Witham,
Essex.

Island Plastics,
Edward Street,
Ryde,
Isle of Wight.

TIMBER

Henry Brown & Sons (Timber) Ltd,
15 Wingfield Road,
Tebworth,
Leighton Buzzard,
Bedfordshire.

Champion (Bromley Boats) Ltd,
Southlands Road,
Bromley,
Kent.

Robbins Ltd,
Cumberland Road,
Bristol BS1 6YU.

ALLOY SPAR KITS

Bowman Boats
54 Beacon Road,
Chatham,
Kent.

TRAILER KITS

Mechanical Services,
Belmont Road,
Bolton,
Lancashire.

Wicksteeds of Royston Ltd,
Meridian Works,
Barkway Road,
Royston,
Hertfordshire.

GLASS FIBRE MATERIALS

Strand Glass Fibre Ltd,
Brentway Trading Estate,
Brentford,
Middlesex.

Ryplas Ltd,
Howard Chase,
Pipps Hill Industrial Estate,
Basildon,
Essex.

SETS OF FITTINGS

W. F. Harrison,
7 Scott Street,
Keighley,
West Yorkshire BD21 2JJ.

Book list

Boat World, Haymarket Publishing Ltd, annually, £4.
Guide to harbours, builders and services.

Build Your Own Boat, Percy Blandford, Stanley Paul, 1971, £3.75.
Plywood boatbuilding.

Encyclopedia of Small Craft Maintenance, Percy Blandford, Pelham, 1978, £5.50.
Looking after your boat.

Instant Weather Forecasting, A. Watts, Adlard Coles, 1966, £2.75.
Short-term local forecasts.

Knots, Splices and Fancy Work, Charles Spencer, Brown, Son and Ferguson, £2.10.
Common practical knots and some decorative work.

Motor Boat and Yachting Manual, T. Cox, Stanford Maritime Ltd, out of print.
Technical information.

Navigation for Yachtsmen, Mary Blewitt, Stanford Maritime Ltd, 1977, £1.95.
Guide to basic navigation.

Nicholson's Guides to the Waterways (4 volumes), David and Charles, £2.25 each.
All British navigable rivers and canals.

Sailing Yacht Design, Douglas Phillips-Birt, Adlard Coles, 1978, £12.
Design, as applied to larger craft.

Sails, Jeremy Howard-Williams, Adlard Coles, 1976, £7.75.
Types, construction and repair.

Sea Signalling Simplified, J. Russell, Adlard Coles, 1976, £2.95.
Methods of visual communications.

Stanford's Sailing Companion, S. Campbell and R. J. Riley, Stanford Maritime Ltd, 1976, £4.95.
General references mainly for cruising yachts.

Start to Navigate, Conrad Dixon, Adlard Coles, 1977, £2.95.
Introductory.

The Broads Book,
The Thames Book,
The Canals Book,
Link House Publications, annually, £1.25 each.
Detailed guide books.

The Sailing Yacht, Juan Baader, Adlard Coles, 1978, £15.
Analysis of yachts and their gear.

This is Sailing, Richard Creagh-Osborne, Nautical, 1972, £3.90.
Comprehensive dinghy sailing.

Where to Launch Your Boat, Link House Publications, annually, 85p.
Guide to launching sites for trailed boats. (Name change from **Getting Afloat.**)

MAGAZINES

Useful magazines to read include:
Boat, Motor Boat and Yachting, Practical Boat Owner, Yacht and Boat

Owner (formerly **Small Boat**), **Yachting Monthly**, **Yachting World** and **Yachts and Yachting**.
These are available monthly from your local newsagent except for **Yachts and Yachting** which is published fortnightly.

Charts and pilot books

The official charts, published by the Hydrographer of the Navy, are mostly intended for larger craft. They can be used for small craft particularly where harbour plans are included or there are no other charts.

Stanford Maritime Ltd, 12 Long Acre, London WC2E 9LP, publish coloured charts with information of particular interest to yachtsmen for the more popular yachting areas. They also publish harbour charts covering the south of England.

Imray, Laurie, Norie and Wilson, St Ives, Huntingdon, publish large-scale charts covering popular areas and smaller-scale charts for longer cruises round most of the British Isles.

For inland cruising, Stanford publish a general map and special maps of the Thames and Norfolk Broads.

A nautical almanac, as well as charts, is needed when cruising on tidal waters. For small boats, the most useful is the annual **Reed's Nautical Almanac** (Thomas Reed Publications Ltd, Saracen's Head Buildings, 36 Cock Lane, London EC1A 9BY).

Pilot books also supplement charts. There are several suitable for yachtsmen. Stanford's Harbour Guides are available for popular areas, while Adlard Coles, Granada Publishing Ltd, Frogmore, St Albans, Hertfordshire AL2 2NF, publish pilot books covering British, French and Baltic waters.

The most comprehensive yachtsman's pilot book, covering most of Europe as well as British waters is **The Cruising Association Handbook**, published by the Cruising Association and also obtainable from the Royal Yachting Association.

There is a large number of other publications covering

© 1976 ANWB Royal Dutch Touring Club

specific areas. Some are produced by local publishers, so it is advisable to seek the advice of a specialist bookseller. One that deals with mail orders is Warsash Nautical Bookshop, 3 Newtown Road, Warsash, Southampton SO3 6FY.

Useful addresses

Royal Yachting Association,
Victoria Way,
Woking,
Surrey GU21 1EQ.
The national body representing sailing and other boating interests.

The Sports Council,
70 Brompton Road,
London SW3 1EX.
The official body co-ordinating sail training among other activities. Works through regional offices.

National Sailing Centre,
Arctic Road,
West Cowes,
Isle of Wight.
Main small boat sailing training facility.

National Water Sports Centre,
Holme Pierrepont,
Nottingham NG12 2LU.
Used for many water activities besides sailing.

National Scout Boating Centre,
Longridge,
Quarry Wood Road,
Marlow,
Buckinghamshire SL7 2RE.
Training centre for members of Scout Association.

Sail Training Association,
Bosham,
Chichester,
Sussex PO18 8HR.
Operators of square-rigged training ships.

Ocean Youth Club,
1 Oak Street,
Gosport,
Hampshire PO12 1JN.
Operators of sailing yachts for youth training.

Royal Society for the Prevention of Accidents,
Royal Oak Centre,
Brighton Road,
Purley,
Surrey CR2 2UR.
Publications on water safety.

National School Sailing Association, Chelstoke,
Lymington Bottom Road,
Medstead,
Alton,
Hampshire.
Federation of school sailing clubs.

CLUBS

There is a very large number of sailing clubs in Great Britain. If you cannot find a suitable one locally get in touch with the Royal Yachting Association or contact one of the following organizations.

Amateur Yacht Research Society,
Hermitage,
Newbury,
Berkshire.
Research and experiment with sailing craft.

Dinghy Cruising Association,
33 Blythe Hill Lane,
London SE6 4UP.
For those who prefer small sailing boat cruising.

Junior Offshore Group,
149 St Pancras,
Chichester,
West Sussex.
Smaller offshore racing yachts.

Old Gaffers Association,
Braeside,
2 Greenbank Street,
Galashiels TD1 3BL.
Enthusiasts for gaff-rigged boats.

CLASS ASSOCIATIONS

For all of the popular classes of sailing boat there are owners' associations. These are additional to clubs which sail the classes, and provide information of mutual interest as well as administer the measuring and numbering of boats in the class. Addresses can be obtained from the RYA.

INLAND WATERWAYS AUTHORITIES

It is necessary to obtain permission before launching a boat where there is no right of way. This is usually by licence from one of these controlling authorities:

British Waterways Board,
Craft Licensing Office,
Willow Grange,
Watford,
Hertfordshire.
Nearly all canals, reservoirs feeding them, the navigable parts of the Severn, Trent, Bristol Avon and some other rivers.

Thames Water Authority,
Nugent House,
Vastern Road,
Reading RG1 8DB.
Thames above Teddington Lock.

Anglian Water Authority,
Great Ouse River Division,
Great Ouse House,
Clarendon Road,
Cambridge CB2 2BL.
Great Ouse, Cam tributaries.

Anglian Water Authority,
Welland and Nene River Division,
North Street,
Oundle,
Peterborough.
Nene and adjoining waters.

Upper Avon Navigation Trust,
Avon House,
Harvington,
Worcestershire.
Stratford Avon up-river of Evesham.

Lower Avon Navigation Trust,
Rose Bank,
Cleeve Prior,
Evesham,
Worcestershire.
Stratford Avon from Evesham to Tewkesbury.

National Trust,
Broadlands,
Norrans Road,
Ambleside,
Cumbria.
Access to many waters in the Lake District.

River Commissioners,
21 South Quay,
Great Yarmouth,
Norfolk NR30 2RE.
Rivers and lakes of Norfolk and Suffolk Broads.

Glossary

Aback: wind striking a sail on the opposite side to normal. Holding the clew of a sail to windward.
Abaft: towards the stern, but outside the boat.
Abeam: direction at right-angles to the centreline of the boat.
About: turn round or change direction, as to go about when tacking to windward.
Adrift: floating unfastened.
Aft: towards the stern or behind the boat.
A-lee: to leeward. Direction to which the wind blows. The helm is a-lee when the tiller is pushed to leeward.
Aloft: in the rigging above deck level.
Amidships: middle of the boat.
Anchor: any type of hook or weight to grip the bottom and attached by a cable to the boat to prevent it drifting. A rond anchor is a single hook for anchoring to a bank.
Astern: behind the boat.
Back: sheet the clew of a sail to windward. The wind backs if it changes direction anti-clockwise.
Backstay: aft support for a mast. A 'permanent backstay' goes to the transom. 'Running backstays' go to each gunwale. One is slackened and the other tightened depending on which side the boom is.
Ballast: weight carried to increase stability. It may be inside the boat or provided in the keel.
Batten: stiffener in the edge of a sail. Usual in leech of a mainsail.
Beam: greatest width of a boat.
Bear away: to alter the direction of the boat more to leeward so the bow goes further away from the wind.
Bearing: direction of an object from the viewer.
Beat: sail to windward, close-hauled.
Belay: secure or make fast anything, particularly a rope.
Bend: fasten a rope or sail to a spar. Type of knot.
Bight: loop of rope. Rope doubled back. Inlet or bay.
Bilge: lower part of a hull.
Block: device containing at least one sheave (pulley wheel) for altering the direction of a rope or using it to provide a purchase.
Bobstay: brace from the end of a bowsprit to a lower point on the stem.
Bollard: strong point for securing a rope. It may be a post ashore or a large type of cleat on the deck.
Bolt rope: rope strengthening the edge of a sail.
Boom: spar along the foot of a sail.
Boom vang: alternative name for a kicking strap, angled from the boom to a lower point on the mast.
Bow: forward part of a boat.
Bowsprit: spar projecting forward from the bow.
Broach to: to swing across a following sea so the boat is broadside to the waves.
Broad reach: sailing with the

wind slightly aft of abeam.
Bulkhead: upright partition across the boat.
Bumkin, bumpkin: spar projecting over the stern to take a backstay or mizzen sheet.
Bunt: central area or body of a sail.
Buoy: any object floating as a marker and anchored to the bottom. It may be a navigational aid, a means of mooring, or an indicator of a racing course.
Buoyancy: force which enables anything to float.
Buoyancy aid: safety garment to keep its wearer afloat, but (in Britain) one without the qualities that permit it to be called a 'lifejacket'.
Burgee: small flag at masthead.
By the lee: wind coming over the same side as the boom, so the sail may be taken aback and caused to gybe.
Cast off: let go a mooring.
Catamaran: twin-hulled craft.
Centreboard (or plate): pivoting keel which raises into a case.
Chain plate (shroud plate): metal fitting on boat side for attachment of mast shroud.
Chine: angle between side and bottom of a hull. Originally 'chime'.
Clawing off: getting away from a potentially dangerous situation, particularly a lee shore.
Cleat: fitting, usually two-pronged, for securing rope.
Clew: lower aft corner of a sail.
Close-hauled: sailing as close as possible towards the wind.
Coaming: protective edge around a cockpit, well or hatchway.
Cockpit: open area normally occupied by the crew below deck level in a yacht.
Cringle: rope loop or eye formed in the bolt rope of a sail or net.
Crosstrees: spreaders over which the shrouds from the top of the mast are arranged.
Cuddy: shelter not large enough to be a cabin.
Cunningham hole: device near the tack of a mainsail for adjusting the fullness of the sail.
Daggerboard (or plate): lifting keel that moves up and down through its case or trunk, instead of pivoting like a centreboard.
Displacement: weight of water which a craft displaces when afloat.
Draft (draught): depth a hull is immersed, from the surface of the water to the lowest point of the hull, keel or other extension.
Ease: let out.
Easy: gently.
Ebb: stream due to the dropping or falling of the tide.
Fairlead: guide for a rope.
Fair wind: following wind before which the yacht runs.
Fall off: turn away from the wind when sailing.
Fender: protective pad fitted round a boat, but sometimes applied to hanging pads, which are more correctly 'fend-offs'.
Flood: tidal stream due to the rising tide.
Foot: bottom edge of a sail.
Forestay: mast support going to the stem, bowsprit or foredeck.
Forward (pronounced 'forrard'): towards the bow.
Free: with the wind abaft the beam.
Freeboard: amount of hull above the waterline.
Full and bye: sailing close-hauled with sails well filled and able to luff. Pinching too close into the wind, then bearing away, possibly to clear an obstruction.
Furl: roll up a sail.
Gaff: spar supporting the head of a four-sided sail, but entirely aft of the mast. If it crosses the mast it is a 'yard'.
Garboard: lowest part of a hull next to the keel. The planks each side of the keel are 'garboard strakes'.
Genoa: large jib sail with considerable overlap on the mainsail.
Go about: change tack to bring wind to the other side.
Gooseneck: universal joint fitting that links the end of the boom to the mast.
Goose-winged: sailing before the wind with the jib held out to the opposite side of the mainsail.
Grommet: rope ring.
Gudgeon: part of a rudder hinge with a hole to take the pintle.
Gunter: type of mainsail in which the gaff continues almost vertically above the mast.
Gunwale: top of the side of a boat.
Guy: line to steady or trim a spar, as with a spinnaker boom.
Gybe: change direction with the wind aft, so the sails are blown across the boat.
Halliard (halyard): rope used to hoist a sail, flag or other gear.
Hank: clip on a sail for attaching to a stay.
Harden a sheet: haul it in.
Headboard: wood or metal plate fixed in the head of a sail.
Heave to: adjust sails and rudder so boat is stopped safely.
Helm: tiller or other steering gear.
Hogged: a boat is hogged if the keel line sags at the ends.
Hoist: haul aloft, also the

perpendicular part of a flag.
Horse: transverse metal, or rope, arrangement on which a slide or traveller attached to a sheet can move.
Hove to: having the sails and rudder arranged so as to keep the boat heading into wind, but stationary or only making slight way through the water. The action is 'heaving to'.
Inboard: within the boat.
In irons: all way lost when attempting to go about on a tack. The boat is pointing into the wind with the sails flapping, but it will not pay off on to either tack by its own momentum and is temporarily out of control.
Jaws: horns on the end of a gaff to fit each side of the mast.
Jib: sail forward of the mast of a sloop.
Keel: lower central member of a hull. Also a projection below the hull to limit sideways movement through the water. Twin projections are 'bilge keels'.
Kicking strap: light tackle angled from the boom to a lower part of the mast, also called a 'boom vang'.
Knee: supporting or strengthening angle bracket, often of wood.
Knot: unit of speed meaning 'nautical mile per hour'. Never 'knots per hour', e.g. '5 knots' means '5 nautical miles per hour'.
Lanyard: thin line holding gear in place. The lashing on the end of a shroud.
Lay: twist of the strands of a rope. Most laid rope has three strands laid up right-handed, meaning that as you look along the rope the strands twist away from you to the right.
Leeboards: alternative to a keel for preventing a boat moving sideways through the water. They are arranged on each side of the hull, but only the one on the leeside is lowered.
Leech: aft edge of a sail.
Lee shore: shore on which the wind is blowing from seaward.
Leeward (pronounced 'loo-ard')**:** away from the direction of the wind, towards the direction in which it is blowing.
Leeway: move sideways through the water in the direction the wind is blowing.
Lifebelt: buoyant device, usually a ring, worn under the armpits.
Lifebuoy: rigid, or semi-rigid, buoyant ring to be thrown to a person in the water.
Lifejacket: buoyant garment. In Britain the name is reserved for one that will turn an insensible person the right way up. Otherwise, it is called a 'buoyancy aid'.
List: lean to one side.
Luff: leading edge of a sail. A boat luffs when it is turned closer to the wind.
Lug: four-sided sail that goes forward as well as aft of the mast.
Make fast: secure, or belay, a rope.
Neap tide: when the tidal range is least—rising less and dropping less than other tides during the four week cycle.
Outhaul: line for extending a sail along a spar.
Painter: rope used for mooring, particularly in a dinghy.
Parrels: small wooden balls, like beads, used on line round the mast with a gaff-headed mainsail.
Pay off: allow the boat to turn to leeward.
Pinching: attempting to sail too close to the wind.
Pintle: part of a rudder hinge that fits into a gudgeon.
Port: left-hand side of a boat when looking forward.
Port tack: sailing with the wind coming over the port bow.
Pram (praam): dinghy without a stem, but the planks meet at a point at gunwale level or on a bow board like a transom.
Pulpit: metal tubular guard rail at the bow.
Pushpit: metal tubular guard rail round the stern.
Quarter: direction between directly astern and abeam is 'on the quarter'. The corner between the gunwale and the transom on each side.
Rake: slope, particularly of a mast.
Reach: sail with the wind abeam, or almost so.
Reef: reduce the area of a sail.
Riding light: white all round light shown when anchored at night.
Rigging screw: tensioner or turnbuckle for shrouds and similar applications with lefthand and righthand threads.
Roach: area between the curved leach of a mainsail and a straight line between head and clew.
Roller reefing: reefing by rolling some of the mainsail round the boom, or the jib round the forestay.
Rowlocks: originally notches through which oars were put, but now applied to the metal fittings for rowing that were called 'crutches'.
Running rigging: all of the ropes that are adjustable and used to hoist or control sails.
Shackle: metal fitting, usually looped with a screw pin, for joining parts together.
Sheave: pulley wheel over which a rope passes.
Sheet: rope used to control a sail.

Shroud: side stay for a mast, secured to the gunwale.
Shroud plate: metal fittings for attachment of a shroud to the side of a boat, also called a 'chain plate'.
Sliding seat: platform that can be extended either side of a small boat, for a crew member to get on to use his weight to trim the boat. Alternative to a trapeze.
Sloop: single-masted craft with a mainsail and one sail forward of the mast.
Spar: any wood or metal bar used to set up or support a sail.
Spinnaker: light parachute-shaped head sail.
Spring tide: tide that has the greatest range in a four-week cycle, rising highest and dropping lowest.
Standing rigging: permanent rigging supporting a mast.
Starboard: right-hand side of a boat when facing forward.
Starboard tack: sailing with the wind coming over the starboard bow.
Stay: support for the mast.
Stern sheets: seat next to the transom in an open boat.
Stern way (or board): sailing backwards, usually unintentionally.
Stiff: having ample stability so as to carry an adequate area of sail without listing unduly.
Strake: plank lengthwise in the hull.
Swig: extra pull on a rope after it is apparently taut, by springing outwards and taking up at the cleat as it is released.
Tabernacle: mounting for a mast on deck or cabin top, which allows the mast to pivot down.
Tack: sail a zig-zag course towards the wind. The lower forward corner of a sail.
Tackle (pronounced 'tayckle'): system of rope and blocks to obtain a mechanical advantage or purchase.
Thimble: round, or heart-shaped, metal piece with a groove round for a rope. Used mainly to prevent wear in a rope loop.
Thwart: crosswise member to provide hull stiffness and forming a seat in a boat. The main thwart is the centre one. A mast thwart supports the mast.
Tiller: forward extension from the top of the rudder to provide a means of controlling it for steering. A tiller extension may hinge on its end for use when the helmsman is sitting out.
Timbers: crosswise frames in a hull.
Topping lift: rope used to support the boom when it is not held by the fully hoisted sail.
Topsides: that part of the hull above water.
Transit: two or more objects observed in line.
Transom: board forming the flat aft end of a hull.
Trapeze: belt/seat arrangement slung from the mast to support a person outboard with his feet on the gunwale, gives greater leverage when using body weight to balance the boat.
Traveller: slide on a track or rod, as when a sheet is arranged to travel across a horse.
Trim: how the boat floats—its attitude.
Trimaran: three-hulled boat.
Turnbuckle: tensioning device using right-hand and left-hand threads for adjustment. Also called a 'rigging screw' when used on shrouds.
Una rig: boat rigged with a single sail.
Up wind: object nearer the direction the wind is coming from than the observer.
Vang: steadying rope.
Veer: turn away from the wind. A wind change clockwise. To veer a cable is to let out more.
Wake: disturbed water left astern.
Warp: strong rope used for anchoring.
Way: momentum through the water. A moving vessel is 'under way'. It is 'under weigh' when the anchor is being weighed, or lifted, but the vessel is not yet moving.
Wear: sailing a circle to change direction downwind to avoid a gybe. May also mean turning away from the wind, as in veer, or has been used to mean a gybe.
Weather: direction from which the wind is blowing (windward), or the part of the boat on that side. Opposite to lee.
Weather helm: tendency for the boat to turn into the wind if the tiller is released. Slight weather helm is desirable as a safety precaution.
Weather shore: shore where the wind is blowing from the land to the sea.
Whipping: binding or serving on the end of a rope to prevent it becoming unlaid.
Winch: mechanical device for exerting extra tension on a rope or chain.
Windlass: type of winch, particularly used for raising an anchor.
Windward: towards the direction from which the wind is blowing.
Yard: spar supporting the top of a four-sided sail, like a gaff, but with part of the spar passing across the mast.
Yaw: swinging from side to side of the intended course unintentionally, particularly when running.

Insignia

Many sailing craft show an emblem or insignia on their mainsail for recognition of their class. The registered number in the class may also be displayed and this is essential for racing. Examples of typical insignia are shown, but there are hundreds more. Clarity at a distance is important in their design.

Lysander
A 5·2-m cruiser, double chine and bilge keels, gunter or Bermudan sloop rig, originally of plywood construction, but some are glass fibre.

Silhouette
A 5·2-m Bermudan sloop cruiser, originally of hard chine plywood construction with twin keels, but Mk III is round-bottomed glass fibre.

Pageant
One of a series of cruisers with similar insignia. This one is 7m long with a Bermudan rig and a round-bottomed glass fibre hull.

International Tornado
Fast 6·1-m catamaran, sloop rig with a fully-battened high aspect-ratio mainsail and a mast on a beam just forward of centre.

Cherub
Fast 3·6-m racing dinghy from New Zealand, hard chine plywood or glass fibre hull (rules allow variations in shape), spinnakers used.

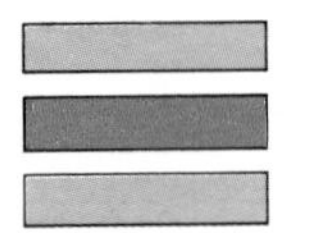

International Contender
High-performance single-hander, 4·9m long, trapeze and single well-battened sail on a bending mast. Low-profile hull may be in any material.

International Enterprise
A 4-m, double-chine racing dinghy, distinctive blue sail, plywood or glass fibre hull. Popular club racer in many parts of the world.

International Finn
4·5-m single-hander, single sail on a bendy mast, round-bottomed hull. Probably the most famous single-hander in the world.

International Fireball
Distinctive, shallow, hard chine hull and flat-bottomed bow, 5m long, originally of plywood construction, but many are glass fibre.

International Flying Dutchman
One of the fastest 1, 2-man centreboard dinghies, 6m long, carries trapeze and spinnaker. Used in the Olympics.

International Five-o-five
Fast, 5·05-m long, two-man racing dinghy, round-bottomed hull flared out at gunwales. British design developed in France.

International 420
(pronounced 'four-twenty') Stable glass fibre hull, 4·20m long, alternative rigs for beginners and racing. French origin.

G.P. 14
Popular 4·3-m craft designed for amateur plywood construction. G.P. stands for 'general purpose', but most boats used for club racing.

Heron
Home-construction, car-top boat, 3·4m long single chine plywood hull, gunter sloop—one of the few classes raced with this rig.

International Laser
Lightweight single-hander, 4·2m long, single Bermudan sail on an unstayed mast, three-quarters decked, daggerboard. Canadian origin.

Lightning
Heavily-built, stable hard chine hull, 5·8m long, strictly one design. Originated in the USA late 1930s, but still widely used and internationally raced.

National Merlin-Rocket
Wood or glass fibre clinker-hulled racer, 4·3m long, top mainsail batten gives leech an angular outline. Popular club racer.

Minisail
Shallow sailing, plywood or glass fibre, surfboard-type hull, 4m long, single Bermudan sail, a small foot well for a cockpit, and a daggerboard.

Mirror
'Stitch and glue' plywood sailing pram, 3·3m long, built from a kit and raced with a gunter sloop rig, red sails. British origin.

International Moth
Single-hander, 3·35m long, developed from several origins so giving many shapes. Sailed worldwide, largest fleet is Australian.

National 12
A restricted class more than forty years old. Allows many variations within the length of 3·66m. Has produced many new ideas, e.g. planing.

International O.K.
A 4-m single-handed racer—an alternative to the Finn—single sail on an unstayed mast with the boom tenoned to it. Danish origin.

International Optimist
Boxy plywood or glass fibre, 2·3-m pram dinghy with a sprit sail. Intended to be raced by a crew of one, aged between 7 and 16. American origin.

Tarpon
Double chine, general-purpose 4·3-m plywood boat, gunter rig, half-decked and a removable cuddy. Used for fishing and cruising/camping.

International Vaurien
Popular French dinghy class, but raced in most European countries. Just over 4m long, first built in plywood, now glass fibre.

Wayfarer
Beamy 4·8-m, partly decked, stable dinghy. Double chine hull originally plywood, but now usually glass fibre. For racing, cruising and training.

Index

Numbers in italics refer to illustrations

Credits

Artwork
Terry Allen Design Ltd/Robert Burns/Rhoda Burns
Sally Launder
David Worth

Photographs
J Allan Cash: 24, 25, 69
Beken of Cowes: 67 (bottom)
Alistair Black: 5, 10, 29 (top right), 44, 57, 67 (top left and top right)
Peter Copley: 6, 52
Linkhouse Publications: 27, 64
Mirror Group Newspapers: 22
Netherlands National Tourist Office: 68, 72
Ronald Sheridan: 4
Roger Smith: 9, 71
Spectrum Colour Library: 59
John Watney, 13, 23, 29, 33, 61, 77, 84

The illustration on page 86 has been copied from the water chart of the Frisian lakes of the Royal Dutch Touring Club ANWB, with the approval of the ANWB.

Cover
Design: Barry Kemp
Photograph: Beken of Cowes